# Improving the Regulatory
# Review Process:
# Assessing Performance
# and Setting Targets

# CMR Workshop Series

Monitoring for Adverse Drug Reactions
*Editors: S.R. Walker and A. Goldberg*

Long-Term Animal Studies
Their Predictive Value for Man
*Editors: S.R. Walker and A.D. Dayan*

Medicines and Risk/Benefit Decisions
*Editor: S.R. Walker and A.W. Asscher*

Quality of Life: Assessment and Application
*Editors: S.R. Walker and R.M. Rosser*

International Medicines Regulations
A Forward Look to 1992
*Editors: S.R. Walker and J.P. Griffin*

Animal Toxicity Studies: Their Relevance for Man
*Editors: C.E. Lumley and S.R. Walker*

Creating the Right Environment for Drug Discovery
*Editor: S.R. Walker*

Current Issues in Reproductive and Developmental Toxicology
Can an International Guideline be Achieved?
*Editors: C.E. Lumley and S.R. Walker*

The Carcinogenicity Debate
*Editors: J.A.N. McAuslane, C.E Lumley and S.R. Walker*

The Relevance of Ethnic Factors in the Clinical Evaluation of Medicines
*Editors: S.R. Walker, C.E Lumley and J.A.N McAuslane*

Improving the Regulatory Review Process: Industry and Regulatory
Initiatives
*Editors: C.E. Lumley and S.R. Walker*

Safety Evaluation of Biotechnologically-derived Pharmaceuticals:
Facilitating a Scientific Approach
*Editors: S.A. Griffiths and C.E. Lumley*

# Improving the Regulatory Review Process: Assessing Performance and Setting Targets

*Edited by*

## Neil McAuslane and Stuart Walker

*Centre for Medicines Research International*
*Carshalton, Surrey, UK*

*Proceedings of a CMR International Workshop held at Nutfield Priory,*
*Nutfield, UK, January 1997*

SPRINGER-SCIENCE+BUSINESS MEDIA, B.V.

A catalogue record for this book is available from the British Library

ISBN 978-94-010-6042-4     ISBN 978-94-011-4874-0 (eBook)
DOI 10.1007/978-94-011-4874-0

**Copyright**

Typeset by Martin Lister Publishing Services, Bolton-le-Sands, Carnforth, Lancs., UK

# Contents

# Preface

The Twelfth International Workshop organised by Centre for Medicines Research International was held at Nutfield Priory in Surrey in January 1997. This two-day meeting brought together invited representatives from the pharmaceutical industry and the regulatory agencies in Europe (Italy, The Netherlands, Germany, EMEA, Sweden, France and the UK), the United States (representatives from both CDER and CBER), Canada, Australia and Japan to discuss assessing performance and setting targets

Setting performance targets is an established practice for the pharmaceutical industry, enabling it to drive performance. At a time when it is common practice for medicines to be developed for a global market and pharmaceutical companies are endeavouring to expedite the drug development process, Regulatory Authorities have also been concentrating on improving their efficiency and effectiveness. Up until now, for most authorities, this has involved only the streamlining of existing processes and this has resulted in marked improvements in approval times for most markets. In order for further improvements to be made, authorities will have to evaluate their processes. There is, therefore, much to be gained from the sharing of ideas, in particular those concerned with best practice.

Currently, measures of performance that are available for making comparisons between agencies differ in their completeness and in what they measure. The FDA is one of the most transparent authorities in terms of making public the statistics on review times and the decisions made. Further, the draft EC Notice to Applicants provides clear performance targets for parts of the Centralised and Mutual Recognition Procedures. In addition, Japan is in the process of making new legislation covering the review process, with a proposed increase in transparency.

Performance measures must reflect more than just speed. However, measuring quality is far more difficult. What systems can therefore be put in place to ensure consistency in quality across therapeutic areas within authorities and across national authorities? It is not surprising that questions are being asked as to how performance might be measured and compared between different authorities who are now often in receipt of dossiers that have been submitted to several agencies at the same time. Issues such as "what target should be set for the review of new medicines?" and "how can quality be assured?" are now considered to be of critical importance. These questions were addressed by those who are actively involved in ensuring the regulatory review system meets the authorities' responsibilities to both the public and industry.

It is important that following such a workshop, the proceedings should be made available to a wider audience, not only in the hope of stimulating debate and discussion on these important topics, but also to encourage further transparency. The editors would like to thank all the authors, chairmen and participants for their contribution to the workshop. The difficult task of bringing the wider discussions together during the Syndicate Sessions was left to the Rapporteurs, Rolf Bass, André Broekmans, John McEwen and Kjell Strandberg, and to the Chairmen, Gottfried Kreutz, Murray Lumpkin, Dann Michols and Vittorio Silano, and to Trevor Jones who chaired this session; their efforts are gratefully acknowledged.

The editors' thanks also go to Brenda Mullinger who has provided so much editorial support for these proceedings. We are indebted to Sandra Cox, whose work as administrator and compiler has made a major contribution to the quality and timeliness of this publication.

It is hoped that some of the spirit of regulatory co-operation seen at this workshop will lead in the future to increased transparency of regulatory activities, and the ability to assess comparable performance across agencies.

*Neil McAuslane*
*Stuart Walker*

# Foreword

Around 1993 the drug review process in Canada was in need of an overhaul. Canada was criticised as being the slowest submission reviewer in the Western World and the Canadian industry claimed that one leading regulatory agency was doing in 58 days what Canada could not do in 1100. Under new management, the Canadian agency reacted. We made setting review targets and enhancing review performance a prime objective of our renewal process. Industry competitiveness was a spur, but equally important was the charge that we were denying Canadians timely access to new medicines. It was not the easiest time to change a corporate culture, but the Government helped. It cut 50% of our appropriations and authorised us to raise a significant portion of our revenue through fees. Industry would not consider fees without commitments to enhanced performance and we could not enhance performance without setting performance standards and measuring our progress against them.

Unfortunately, we had little information (and even less time) by which to set those standards. We looked abroad to the experience of our sister agencies, but found a confusing array of targets and claims. Several of our colleagues were only just starting down this road and amongst those who had some experience, there was little commonality of process, decision rules, or measurement. Some reported only scientific review times, others the full process to a decision. Some reported time to first decision, others reported the full time to market. There was no agreement even on the measuring stick – calendar or working days!

Left largely to our own devices, we set interim performance standards, reassured our scientists that measuring their performance against those standards would not be the end of the world, augmented our review process with several high technology tools, set up the necessary tracking and monitoring systems, and entered the brave new world of a managed submission review process. We have done relatively well in a short period of time, having halved our average review time, reduced our targets, increased six-fold the number of submissions approved during the first review, and fees now cover 70% of our budget.

However, we are not yet satisfied with the result and we have concerns and questions. How do we ensure that we do not sacrifice decision making quality in the quest for decision-making efficiency? How does a lesser-resourced small agency remain internationally competitive without compromising the health and safety of its citizens? How does one standardise reporting internationally the variables and processes to gain some insight into the experience and performance of the various regulatory regimes? How should this information be collected and interpreted internationally? What is industry's role in the enhancement of both review effectiveness and efficiency? What have other agencies learned that we can use?

In a timely fashion, CMR International has stepped into the fray. In January 1997, it offered a unique and useful opportunity for those in industry and the major regulatory agencies to share their experience and musings. This publication is the result. Terry Eaves and Emily Donnelly speak compellingly on why industry believes regulatory speed is important. Fernand Sauer presents his view on globalisation from a regulator's perspective. Kathy Zoon relates the US FDA experience and reminds us of the need to ensure quality assurance and constant review. Yoshinobu Hirayama lays out the changes taking place in the MHW to bring it up to international standards. The Canadian experiences are illustrated by Beth Pieterson who reiterates the necessity and challenges of finding common, measurable comparators. John McEwen reminds us of the role that quality submissions with adequate data and disclosure play in enhancing the efficiency and effectiveness of the regulator. Rolf Bass details the remarkable progress the EMEA has made in a short period of time.

But improving the regulatory process is not only about increasing efficiency and removing unnecessary barriers to industry competitiveness. It is also about better protecting the health and safety of consumers and enhancing the decision making of health professionals. David Jefferys and Murray Lumpkin highlight the sometimes overlooked element of regulatory effectiveness – the necessity for quality decisions – presenting a far more difficult challenge in performance measurement.

CMR International has activities under way to facilitate comparisons of international regulatory efficiency. Kate Thomas outlines the results of a study initiated to identify the key milestones in the review processes of the major drug regulatory agencies. Identifying common milestones is an essential first step towards a full-scale benchmarking study. She points out that further development will require collaboration between companies and regulatory authorities to gather the data needed to make comparisons, to learn from past successes, and to encourage best practices.

*Dann M Michols*
Director General
Therapeutic Products Directorate
Health Canada
December 1997

# Notes on Contributors and Chairmen

**Professor Rolf Bass MD** is Head of Unit for Human Medicines at the European Agency for the Evaluation of Medicinal Products (EMEA), a position he has held since April 1995. From 1979 until 1995 he was Head of Drug Toxicology and Director and Professor at the Federal Institute for Drugs and Medical Devices in Berlin. From 1984 until 1991 he was Chairman of the Safety Working Party of the Committee for Proprietary Medicinal Products (CPMP) of the European Communities. He has published over 150 papers in the areas of mitochondriogenesis, pre- and postnatal toxicology, transplacental pharmacokinetics, toxicological requirements for safety assessment of drugs for registration, safety requirements for biotechnology products, animal experimentation, formaldehyde, risk assessment and risk management and regulatory affairs.

**André Broekmans MD PhD** is Executive Director of the Medicines Evaluation Board, in the Netherlands. Prior to becoming the Executive Director, he held the post of Head of Department of Clinical Assessment of the Medicines Evaluation Board and between 1987 and 1990, Head of Medical Affairs at the Netherlands Heart Foundation. Dr Broekmans is a member of the Pharmaceutical Committee of the European Commission and a member of the Management Board of the European Medicines Evaluation Agency. He is currently Chairman of the Pharmaceutical Evaluation Report Scheme.

**Emily Donnelly BSc (Pharm) MPSI MR PharmS** is Director and Senior Vice President, Transnational Regulatory Affairs and Compliance at SmithKline Beecham Pharmaceuticals. She has responsibility worldwide for all regulatory activities and compliance and is a member of many SmithKline Beecham Pharmaceuticals Management Committees. She has worked in the pharmaceutical industry for 26 years and is a member of both the Pharmaceutical Society of Ireland and the Royal Pharmaceutical Society of Great Britain. As a pharmacist, Emily Donnelly's experience includes working in quality control, manufacturing, formulation development and as a medical representative. She has also worked in wholesale pharmacy, retail and hospital pharmacy. She spent 5 years with the ABPI working on Scientific, Medical and Regulatory activities and has worked for Leo Pharmaceuticals and Merrell Dow Pharmaceuticals. Miss Donnelly was actively involved in the merger of SmithKline and Beckman and Beecham Pharmaceuticals.

**Terry Eaves BSc PhD FRPharmS CChem FRSC** is currently Director of Group Development Operations for Glaxo Wellcome. He studied Pharmacy at the University of Leeds before completing his PhD at Nottingham University in 1971. Following drug research and development roles in Sandoz, Hoechst, and Merrell Dow he joined Glaxo in 1985 as Development Director. In 1995 he became Senior Vice President and Director of the Glaxo Research Institute in North Carolina after which, in 1996, he returned to London as Worldwide Development Director of the newly merged Glaxo Wellcome company. Dr Eaves is a Fellow of the Royal Pharmaceutical Society, a Chartered Chemist and Fellow of the Royal Society of Chemistry and currently chairs the Research and Development Committee of the ABPI.

**Yoshinobu Hirayama PhD** is currently Manager of the Clinical Trials Advice Division of the Clinical Trials Department of the Organization for Drug ADR Relief, R&D Promotion and Product Review (the Drug Organization). From 1992 to 1996, Dr Hirayama was Deputy Director of the Pharmaceuticals and Cosmetics Division of the Pharmaceutical Affairs Bureau of the Ministry of Health and Welfare (MHW) and from 1988 to 1992, was Deputy Director of the Health Economics Division of the Health Insurance Bureau of the MHW. Prior to that, Dr Hirayama had been an Expert of the Life Science Division of the Research and Development Bureau of the Science and Technology Agency and also in the Food Chemistry Division of the Environmental Health Bureau of the MHW. Dr Hirayama attended the Pharmaceutical Department of Kyoto University in 1971 and graduated in 1980 with a PhD in Pharmaceutical Science.

**David B Jefferys BSc MD FRCP FRCP(Ed) FFPM** is Director, Licensing Division, at the Medicines Control Agency, UK. He is a physician by training and held various posts in clinical and academic medicine before joining the Department of Health in 1984. He worked on the review of medicines and in pharmacovigilance before becoming the Principal Medical Officer in charge of new drug licensing in 1986 and became Business Manager in charge of new drugs and European licensing in 1989 with the creation of the Medicines Control Agency. He is a past Chairman of the Pharmaceutical Evaluation Report Scheme. He is one of the UK members of the CPMP and was the Chairman of the Operational Working Party of the former CPMP. Dr Jefferys is Visiting Professor in Medicine at the University of Newcastle.

**Professor Trevor Jones BPharm PhD FPS CChem FRSC FKC MCPP FFPM** is Director-General of the ABPI, a position he has held since August 1994. He directs all the activities relating to the UK pharmaceutical industry, including government relations, on behalf of 100 national and international pharmaceutical companies. Professor Jones is a member of the UK Government Pharmaceutical Industry Strategy Working Group on pharmaceutical affairs and is on the Board of the International Federation of Pharmaceutical Manufacturers Associations

(IFPMA). From 1987–1994 Professor Jones was a main board director of Wellcome plc, the UK-based pharmaceuticals company, where he was responsible for development of new products, including Zovirax, AZT, Lamictal and Tracruim.

**Professor Gottfried Kreutz Dr Med Dipl Chem** is Director and Professor, and currently head of the Department of Clinical Pharmacology (clinical evaluation, selected therapeutic areas and biometrics) at the Federal Institute for Drugs and Medical Devices (BfArM), Berlin, Germany. Professor Kreutz has received degrees in Medicine from the Free University, Berlin, and in Chemistry from the Technical University, Berlin, and completed postgraduate training in Clinical Pharmacology and Pharmacology/Toxicology before he was recruited to the Federal Health Office in October 1984 as head of the Department of Pharmacovigilance. In November 1993 he became head of the Department of Experimental and Clinical Pharmacology, a position he held for 3 years prior to the re-organisation of BfArM in November 1996. After many years at Free University, Berlin, Professor Kreutz is currently teaching clinical pharmacology/therapeutics at Rudolf Virchow Klinikum of Humboldt University. He has published articles in scientific journals and books, mainly in the areas of clinical toxicology, drug metabolism and pharmacoepidemiology. For many years he has been editing the pharmacovigilance section of the *Federal Health Gazette*, and is a member of the Editorial Board of *Pharmacoepidemiology and Drug Safety*.

**Cyndy Lumley BSc PhD** is Associate Director at Centre for Medicines Research International. Dr Lumley joined the Centre in 1983 after obtaining a BSc in Medical Biochemistry from the University of Surrey and a PhD in Radiation Biology from the University of London. Currently she has overall responsibility for the Centre's research programme, which covers R&D strategies, R&D benchmarking, and regulatory issues, and has an active role in the management of the Unit. Dr Lumley is Chairman of the British Toxicology Society Executive Committee, a member of the American College of Toxicology, on the Editorial Board of *TEN* and is an active contributor to scientific publications and meetings.

**Murray MacIntyre Lumpkin MD MSc** is presently the Deputy Center Director (Review Management) for the Center for Drug Evaluation and Research of the US Food and Drug Administration (FDA). Dr Lumpkin received his baccalaureate degree from Davidson College in 1975 and his medical doctorate degree from Wake Forest University in 1979. His postgraduate education was varied and his professional certifications include paediatrics and tropical medicine. Prior to his present appointment at the FDA, his professional experience included time as a clinical worker in a refugee camp in Bangladesh; a 3-year appointment as chief of paediatric infectious diseases at East Tennessee Children's Hospital in Knoxville; and a 2-year appointment as Medical Director at Abbott Laboratories in Chicago where he was in a senior leadership position on the multi-disciplinary, global team responsible for the worldwide development of a new antimicrobial. In

December 1989, Dr Lumpkin was recruited to the Food and Drug Administration as Director of the Division of Anti-Infective Drug Products. This was one of ten new drug review divisions within the Center for Drug Evaluation and Research of the FDA at that time. In August 1993, he took up his current position and his main responsibilities include oversight and management of the five Offices of Drug Evaluation and their now 15 new drug review divisions, the Office of Epidemiology and Biostatistics, and the Advisory Committee staff in the Center for Drug Evaluation and Research. In addition, he is responsible for the creation and implementation of management initiatives to assure that the Center meets its product review performance goals established in conjunction with the Prescription Drug User Fee Act of 1992.

**Neil McAuslane BSc MSc PhD** is Research Manager at Centre for Medicines Research International, with responsibility for managing the R&D strategies, R&D benchmarking, and regulatory issues programmes. He joined the Centre in 1988 as a Postdoctoral Fellow in affiliation with the Division of Clinical Pharmacy, University of Wales, Cardiff, and became a permanent member of staff in 1991. Dr McAuslane received his PhD degree in Clinical Pharmacology from the University of Edinburgh, having gained an MSc in Toxicology at the University of Surrey and a BSc in Pharmacology from Dundee University. He has edited five books and co-authored several of the Centre's publications and reports.

**John McEwen MB BS MSc MPS** is Head of Evaluation Unit 2, in the Drug Safety and Evaluation Branch, Therapeutic Goods Administration, Australia. The Evaluation Unit is responsible for vaccines and antibiotics and other anti-infective agents, as well as several other classes of drugs. Dr McEwen graduated in Pharmacy at the Victorian College of Pharmacy and obtained an MSc in Neurophysiology at Melbourne University. After a period as lecturer in Physiology, he completed medical training and house positions at Royal Melbourne Hospital. From 1979 to 1989, John McEwen was Secretary of the Adverse Drug Reactions Advisory Committee and subsequently Head, Drug Evaluation Support Branch. During this time he was a member and later Chairman of the Advisory Board to the WHO Collaborating Centre for International Drug Monitoring, based in Uppsala, Sweden, and also acted as Editor of *Australian Prescriber*. He then spent five years as Medical Director, CSL Limited, Melbourne, before taking up his current position in September 1994.

**Dann Michols MBA BComm(Hons)** is currently head of Health Canada's Therapeutic Products Directorate. Mr Michols came to the Department of Health on assignment as Assistant Deputy Minister, National Pharmaceuticals Strategy. His responsibilities were to facilitate federal/provincial initiatives in the area of national pharmaceutical policy and regulation and to co-ordinate the results into a comprehensive and cohesive pharmaceutical policy for Canada. In January 1993, Mr Michols assumed the additional responsibility for the management of Canada's drug review agency and for the implementation of the Gagnon Report recommendations and other similar exercises leading to a renewed Drugs Programme. On 1$^{st}$ January 1997, Health Canada's responsibilities for drug regulation and medical device regulation were merged and the new Therapeutic Products Directorate was created. Prior to his work with the Department, Mr Michols was Director of Operations for the federal Royal Commission on New Reproductive Technologies, responsible for the development and management of all consultation, communication, co-ordination and policy analysis activities. Mr Michols has had a 27-year career in the Canadian Public Service, the last 12 years at the level of Assistant Deputy Minister. He has served as a senior management advisor to UNESCO in Paris and as Assistant Secretary General of the National Museums Corporation of Canada.

**Beth Pieterson MSc MHA** is the Associate Director of the Bureau of Biologics and Radiopharmaceuticals, Therapeutic Products Directorate, Health Canada. Since joining the Therapeutic Products Programme in 1990, Ms Pieterson has worked in operational, policy and management positions. As Chief of the Submissions and Information Policy Division for approximately three years, Ms Pieterson was responsible for co-ordinating the submission process and developing the associated policies, performance targets, and information systems. Ms Pieterson joined the Bureau of Biologics and Radiopharmaceuticals as the Associate Director in April 1996.

**Fernand Sauer** is the Executive Director of the European Agency for the Evaluation of Medicinal Products (EMEA) in London. He is a qualified pharmacist from the University of Strasbourg. He subsequently received a Masters in European and International Law from the University of Paris and various postgraduate diplomas in public health, pharmaceutical legislation and European Community Studies. From 1972 to 1979 Mr Sauer held various positions in France as hospital pharmacist and pharmaceutical inspector at the Ministry of Health. In 1979 he joined the European Commission in Brussels (DG III) as Administrator and in 1985 he became Head of Pharmaceuticals. He has been involved in the completion of the European Internal Market, trilateral harmonisation of regulatory requirements (ICH) between the EC, the USA and Japan and the development of pricing transparency and industrial policy in the pharmaceutical sector.

**Professor Vittorio Silano MSc PhD** is the Director General of the Department for Medicines Evaluation and Pharmacovigilance, Ministry of Health, Italy. Before joining the Ministry of Health, he worked for more than 20 years at the National Institute of Health (Istituto Superiore di Sanità) where for several years he was Director of the Department of Comparative Toxicology. From 1972 to 1981, Professor Silano was a lecturer within the Faculty of Pharmacy, University of Rome, and from 1982 to 1985 he taught in the Postgraduate School of Toxicology of the Faculty of Pharmacy, University of Milan. In 1991 and 1992 he was contract Professor of Nutritional Biochemistry in the Faculty of Medicine of the 2$^{nd}$

University in Rome, and currently he is Professor of Health Legislation at the University of Rome. Professor Silano has collaborated intensely as an expert with numerous international organisations, such as the World Health Organization (for which he worked as a consultant in toxicology in 1982), the Commission of the European Community (for which, up to 1987, he was Chairman of the Scientific Committee for Food), the Council of Europe (for which he collaborated with various teams of experts in the toxicology of flavouring and cosmetic products) and for the Organization for Economic Development and Co-operation (as chairman of various bodies). From June 1991 to March 1992 he also directed the Rome Division of the European Centre on "Environment and Health" for the World Health Organization. He is currently a member of the recently-established European Community Scientific Steering Committee. Professor Silano's scientific output consists of 190 scientific publications, appearing mainly in international scientific journals; these are mostly original results in the area of biochemistry and toxicology, as well as in the field of environmental chemistry. He is also the author of five books and 24 technical reports, as well as being the scientific editor of three books.

**Professor Kjell Strandberg PhD MD** is Director General of Medical Products Agency, Sweden, a position he has held since July 1990. He has been a lecturer in clinical pharmacology and pulmonary medicine, Head of the Pharmacotherapeutic Division, and Director of the Department of Drugs, National Board of Health and Welfare, as well as Head of the Division of Clinical Pharmacology, University Hospital, Uppsala, Sweden. He is a member of the Nordic Council of Medicine, the Royal Swedish Academy of Engineering Sciences, the EU Pharmaceutical Committee and the EU Committee for Proprietary Medicinal Products (CPMP). He has published papers in allergology, pharmacology, clinical pharmacology and drug control.

**Kate Thomas BSc MSc** is a Research Associate within the Regulatory Issues team at Centre for Medicines Research International. She joined the Centre in November 1993, after completing an MSc degree in Clinical Pharmacology at the University of Aberdeen, and a BSc in Pharmacology and Physiology at the University of Leeds. Her current areas of research include the evaluation of regulatory processes and review times for new pharmaceutical compounds, and the impact of the International Conferences on Harmonisation (ICH) on the clinical drug development processes of pharmaceutical companies. She has presented at various international scientific conferences and meetings, and has authored several of the Centre's publications and reports.

**Professor Stuart R Walker BSc PhD(Lond) CChem CBiol FRSC FIBiol FInstD FRCPath** is the Director of Centre for Medicines Research International in the UK and Honorary Professor of Pharmaceutical Medicine, University of Wales, Cardiff. He spent ten years at London University which included lectureships in biochemical pharmacology at St Mary's Hospital Medical School and in clinical pharmacology at the Cardiothoracic Institute in London. This was followed by eight years with Glaxo Group Research in the UK where he had international responsibility for several of their clinical research programmes. His current research interests include studies concerned with improving productivity, efficiency and decision making in global drug development and the regulatory review process as well as public policy issues that relate to these research activities. During his research career, Professor Walker has co-authored over 150 research papers and edited 16 books in the fields of toxicology, clinical development and regulatory policies.

**Kathryn C Zoon PhD** became Director of the Center for Biologics Evaluation Research (CBER), Food and Drug Administration in March 1992. Dr Zoon was formerly the Director of the Division of Cytokine Biology in CBER, where she was actively involved with regulatory issues related to cytokines, growth factors and studies on interferon purification, characterisation and interferon receptors. Dr Zoon worked at NIH from 1975 to 1980, with Nobel Prize Laureate Christian B Anfinsen on the production and purification of human interferons. She received her BS degree, *cum laude*, in Chemistry from Rensselaer Polytechnic Institute in 1970 and was granted a PhD in Biochemistry from The Johns Hopkins University in 1976. Dr Zoon is an editor of the *Journal of Interferon Research* and the author of numerous scientific papers on interferons. She has received numerous awards, including the NIH Lectureship 1994, Sydney Riegelman Lectureship 1994, Biopharm Person of the Year Award 1992, Genetic Engineering News (GEN) Award 1994 for streamlining and improving the regulatory process for biologics and biotechnology products, and the Meritorious Executive Rank Award 1994 for sustained superior performance in revitalising and re-organising the Center for Biologics Evaluation and Research to meet the challenges of new responsibilities and new technologies.

# 1 Assessing performance and setting targets

TERRY EAVES

**Summary**

1. Dramatic changes are leading towards a 'third generation' of pharmaceutical research and development, which will be global, outward looking and driven by technology, genetics and a variety of partnerships.

2. Value for money will become the driver in the marketplace. However, the medicines of tomorrow will be judged on their ability to increase value to the patient and the payor, both therapeutically and financially.

3. In such an environment there will be a need for the skilful use of strategic targets and performance management. Less accessible markers of progress, such as behavioural issues, should not be overlooked in the bid to identify and adopt best practices.

4. More fruitful and flexible collaboration between industry and the regulators will allow mutual learning in these areas, as well as in the more tangible business of new drug development.

## A view of industry

The technological changes that are taking place in the way that we discover and develop drugs are so dramatic that they are leading us towards 'the third generation' of pharmaceutical research and development (Table 1.1).

**Table 1.1 Science/Medicine/Technology**

| | | | | | |
|---|---|---|---|---|---|
| **SCIENCE** | | | | | |
| **First** | | **Second** | | **Third** | |
| Chemistry | + | Biology | + | Genetics | |
| *In vivo* | + | *in vitro* | + | *in silico* | |
| Serendipity | + | Empiricism | + | Prediction | |
| **MEDICINE** | | | | | |
| **First** | | **Second** | | **Third** | |
| Art form | + | Experience-based | + | Evidence-based | |
| Safe | + | Effective | + | Value | |
| Palliation | + | Disease modification | + | Prevention and cure | |
| **TECHNOLOGY** | | | | | |
| **First** | | **Second** | | **Third** | |
| Manual | + | Automated | + | Computer-controlled miniaturised robotics | |
| Small molecules Natural products | + | Recombinant proteins | + | Gene therapy Antisense etc. | |

The first generation which began well over 20 years ago was based on innovative chemistry coupled with thorough *in vivo* evaluation and a great deal of serendipity! This was followed by a second period of more rational molecular drug design based on an improved, but still empirical, understanding of biology. The third generation of research and development will now incorporate, additionally, a profound appreciation of the genetic predisposition for disease and will identify many innovative molecular targets for which new technologies, such as combinatorial chemistry and high throughput screening, will deliver drug candidates. The outcome will be a much greater number of active agents, from which the easiest ones to develop can be systematically selected.

Similar changes have taken place over the same period in medicine and each of the sciences (see Table 1.1). Medicine, once seen as an art form using safe, palliative therapy, has moved through experience-based use of effective second generation drugs to an evidence-based era where there is greater emphasis on value for money for the prevention and even cure of disease. By the same token, the technology to develop drugs has marched forward, from a manual base through automation, to miniaturisation and robotics, which are optimising the approach to drug discovery. All in all, we are on the brink of a revolution in drug research and development.

**The marketplace as driver**

The new approach to pharmaceutical research and development will be fuelled by the need for greater productivity and efficiency and triggered by radical changes that are occurring in the pharmaceutical marketplace. To some extent the marketplace is driving these changes, since science and technology are providing the opportunity but the market is reinforcing the requirement (Table 1.2).

During the first generation, quality products were produced on a regional basis by companies primarily operating in their own domain and growing from within. These companies have now spread to the developed world and are consolidating through

**Table 1.2  Marketplace/Information and regulation**

### MARKETPLACE

| First | | Second | | Third |
|---|---|---|---|---|
| Quality | + | Cost | + | Value |
| Local economy | + | Developed world | + | Global economy |
| Organic growth | + | Mergers and acquisitions | + | Alliances Consortia Joint ventures Spin outs Academic links |

### INFORMATION AND REGULATION

| First | | Second | | Third |
|---|---|---|---|---|
| Library | + | Dedicated system | + | The Internet |
| *Laissez faire* | + | Tight regulation | + | Partnership |

mergers and acquisitions. In the new marketplace, the economy will be truly global; this will spawn greater links into academia, smaller companies, consortia, joint ventures and so forth.

The future of research and development will undoubtedly be global in nature, driven by genetics and new technologies, epitomised by partnerships and dependent on readily available quality information. The new medicines of the future will be judged not only on safety and efficacy considerations but also on their ability to increase value to the patient and payor, both therapeutically and financially.

### Implications for the regulatory environment

When speculating on the implications for the regulatory environment it is worth considering what is happening in the field of information (Table 1.2). A chaotic environment is likely to emerge as ubiquitous, uncensored information on the Internet supplements the current dedicated information systems. In such an environment the creators, producers and regulators of medicines will have to work constructively together.

Not only will the third generation of pharmaceutical research and development require a good understanding of the underlying sciences and technologies, it will also demand a more fruitful and flexible collaboration between the industry and the regulatory agencies. This partnership should extend beyond the very tangible business of new drug development to embrace mutual learning in the important business of defining and monitoring performance targets and learning from best practices.

**Performance targets**

The major components of a good performance target are the task itself, its speed, quantity, standard or quality and its cost. Alone these elements are not sufficient; there is also a need to incorporate continuous improvement and monitor the rate of improvement of desired outcome. In other words, a mechanism is needed for checking that the target is leading in the right direction.

The following statements are all top level performance targets:

*In 1994 Pfizer will have six NCEs in Phase III rising to an impressive 14 by the end of 1995. This is a record for Pfizer and to the best of my knowledge, the industry.*

John Niblack (Executive Vice President, Pfizer)
25 October 1994

*To paraphrase a recent remark by my counterpart at Pfizer, in 1994 SB will have seven NCEs and four novel vaccines in Phase II rising to 20 by the end of 1995. This is a record for SB, and to the best of my knowledge, the industry.*

George Poste (President, R&D, SmithKline Beecham)
12 December 1994

*Glaxo Wellcome has set itself the target of bringing three new medicines per annum to the market from the year 2000.*

James Niedel (Executive Director R&D, Glaxo Wellcome)

November 1995

The last quotation from James Niedel, of my own company, sets an aggressive target based on component targets for the functions which together would deliver an output of three new medicines per annum (Table 1.3). These figures illustrate the importance of flow; for instance, in the review of applications, performance targets *per se* are of little use unless there is a flow of intermediate deadlines throughout the whole process.

**Table 1.3  What Glaxo Wellcome must achieve...**

**What Glaxo Wellcome must achieve...**

| 20 | 60–80 | 15 | 3 |
|---|---|---|---|
| new targets per annum from exploratory research ➡ | projects on a 3–4 year cycle 75% success rate ➡ | candidates per annum 20% success rate in development ➡ | medicines per annum |
| | | | **... more, better, faster** |

A more ambitious approach (Table 1.4) was adopted by George Poste, SmithKline Beecham (Poste, 1994) when he provided targets for average development times. This more realistic outlook indicates that with present technologies development times are unlikely to fall below 5 years.

**Efficiency in R&D**

In its quest for 'best practices' the industry has embraced information generated by CMR International on efficiencies in the drug research and development process. The first of two questionnaire-based reviews (Drasdo and Lumley, 1995a) defined the timepoints generally used for determining elapsed time and identified those

**Table 1.4  Power development – Target 2000 (SmithKline Beecham)**

**Reducing cycle time in new product development**

| Product registrations filed in: | Average duration of development days (years) | | Percentage reduction from baseline |
|---|---|---|---|
| 1989–92 | 3698 | (10.1) | — |
| 1993–94 | 3348 | (9.1) | 10 |
| 1994–95 | 2449 | (6.9) | 33 |
| 1996–97 (est) | 2221 | (6.1) | 40 |
| Target | 2000 | (5.4) | 46 |

Based on Poste 1994, with permission.

that are most important, most easily accessible and most commonly used. Figure 1.1 shows that of the milestones used for tracking speed of development, most companies considered the intervals from GLP toxicity to Phase I studies and from Phase III to submission to be of greatest value.

On the issue of productivity the survey revealed that the number of compounds submitted or the number approved were regarded as better indicators of productivity than the number of compounds synthesised. Most companies were introspective, using only in-house data for reference although some made productivity comparisons with the top ten companies in Phase II and Phase III studies. The quality of in-house research capabilities, decision making and portfolio management were the key factors chosen by most respondents as having greatest impact on successful drug development.

The pilot study for the second review (Drasdo and Lumley, 1995b), which focuses on cycle times from synthesis of a new drug to market, is now complete. The overall purpose is to define performance targets and provide a yardstick for ongoing process improvement and re-design initiatives. To do this, the complex process of drug development is analysed by 'macro' benchmarks (Figure 1.2) to evaluate the whole process and 'micro' benchmarks (Figure 1.3) which look in more detail at the clinical trials process.

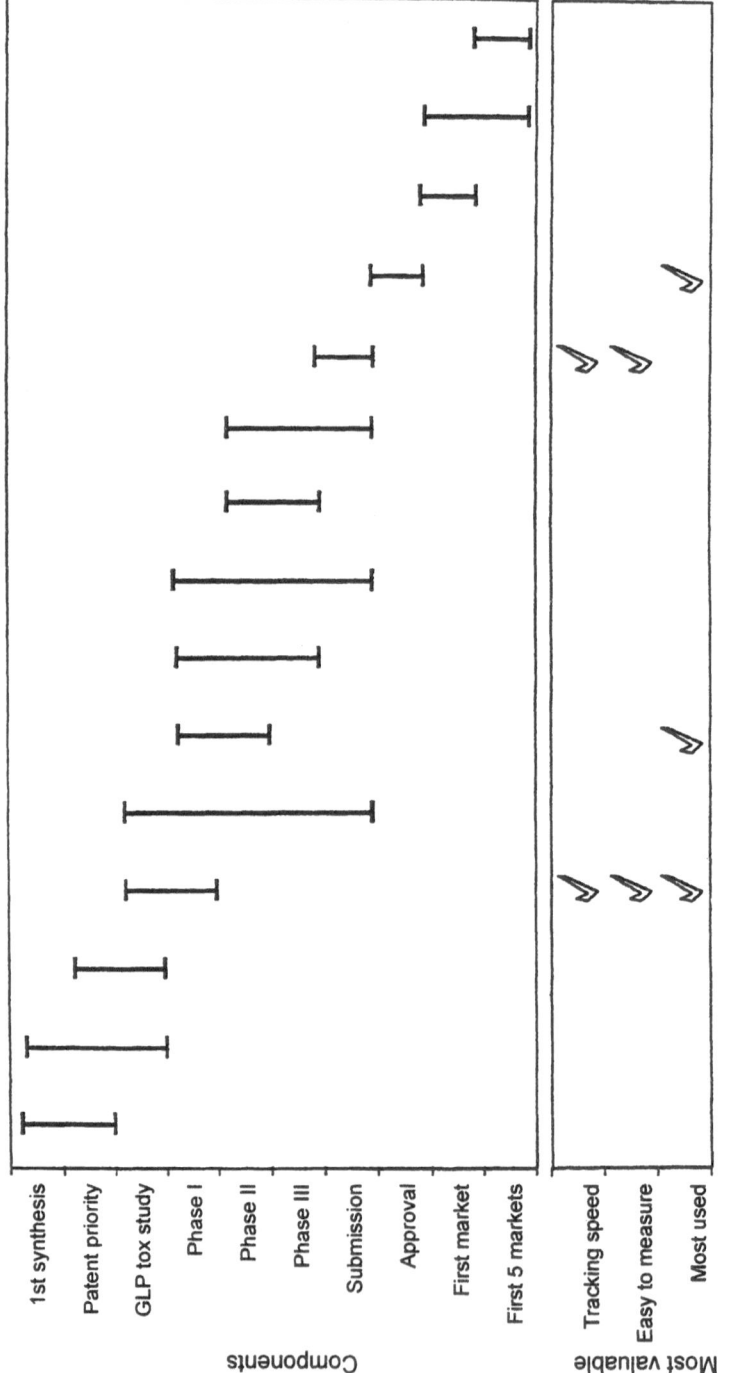

Figure 1.1  Milestones used for tracking speed (Source: CMR International)

8

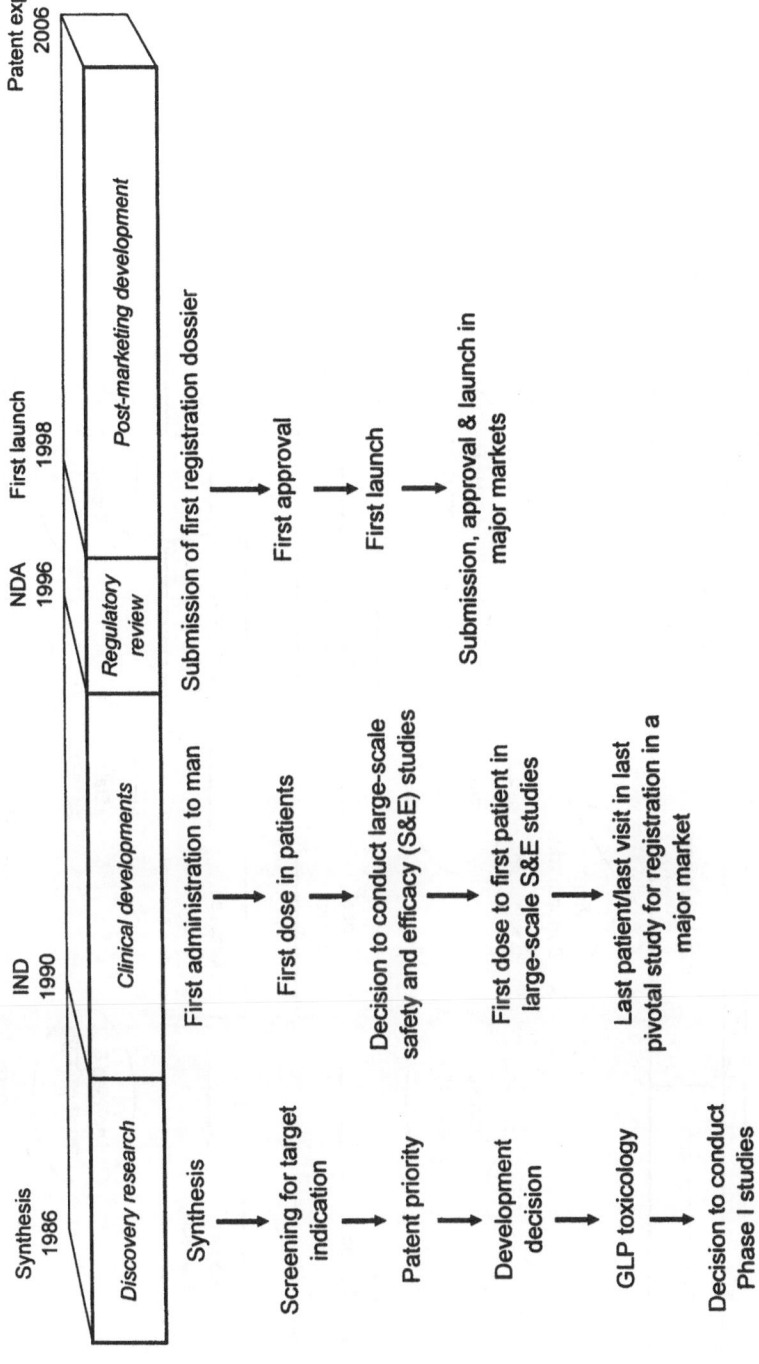

**Figure 1.2** Macro benchmarks in drug development (Source: CMR International)

9

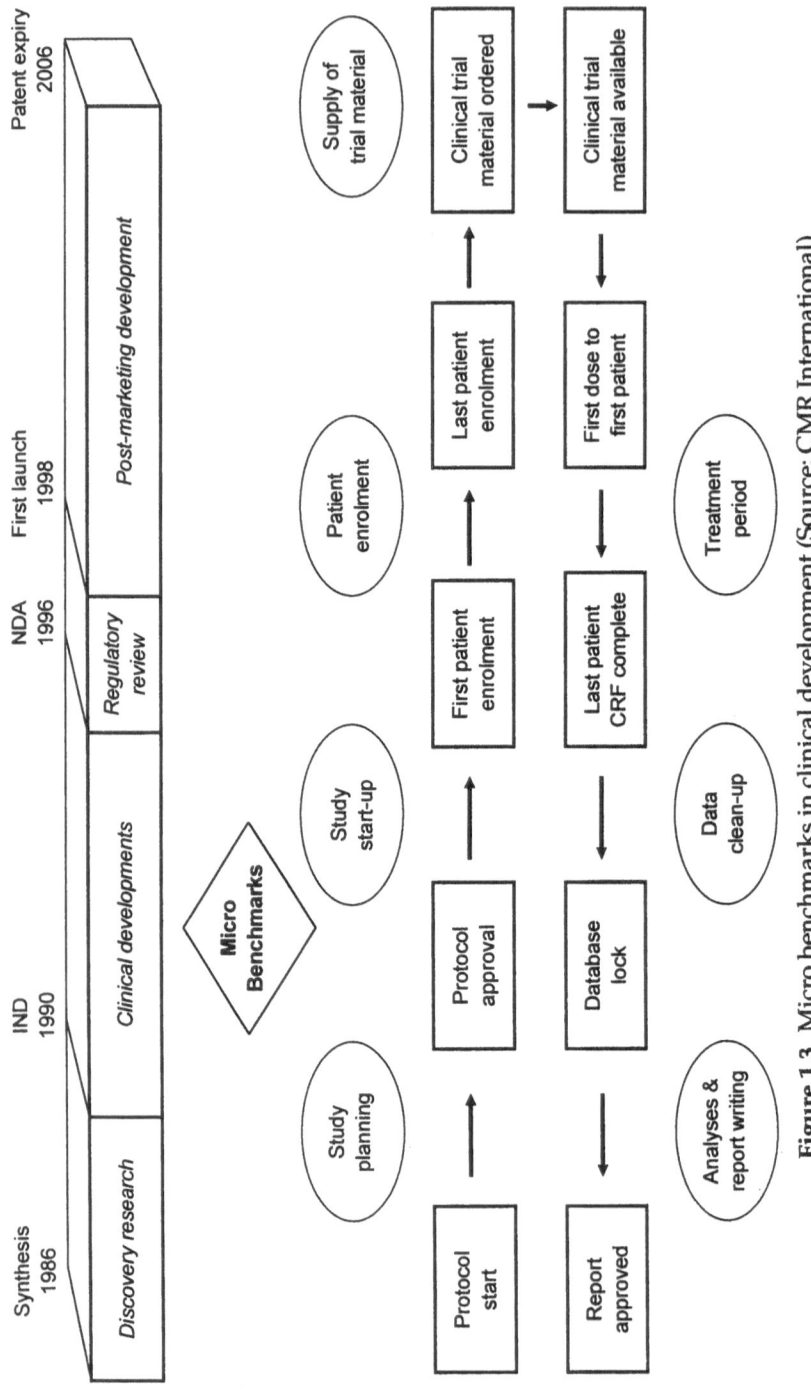

**Figure 1.3** Micro benchmarks in clinical development (Source: CMR International)

**Table 1.5  DELTA behaviours**

---

- **Decision Making** – High-quality decisions are made, explained and evaluated by most capable people

- **Employee Development and Retention** – People feel appreciated, challenged, motivated, recognised and rewarded

- **Leadership** – Leaders are champions, providing direction, motivation, encouragement and support

- **Teamwork** – People work in a high-performance environment where teamwork thrives and where individuals and teams clearly understand their contributions to business goals and objectives

- **Action** ........ DELTA 2000

---

## Performance management

Apart from these very tangible performance measures there are other, less accessible, markers of progress which are overlooked at a price to the organisation. Behavioural issues such as decision making, employee development and retention, leadership qualities and teamwork were revealed as prime concerns amongst the workforce of Glaxo Wellcome. Many of these issues will be addressed through the DELTA 2000 initiative (Table 1.5).

Many pharmaceutical companies are looking way beyond their bounds, to industries as broad ranging as IT, automotives, utilities, foods and airlines, to identify 'best practice' companies in other industrial sectors. The purpose is to tease out various themes that explain why a particular company represents the elite in a specific process or function. Such process themes might include setting common goals, managing to high performance, careful selection and staffing of teams, significant training and education input and adequate rewards and recognition. The implications for the pharmaceutical industry are to ensure that all are challenged to perform well and thus provide a positive impact on the regulatory review process.

## References

Drasdo AL and Lumley CE (1995a). Efficiency in R&D: Key Benchmarks. Centre for Medicines Research International Report, CMR 95-50R, July 1995.

Drasdo AL and Lumley CE (1995b). Benchmarking for Efficient Drug Development. Report of Industry Discussion Meeting. Centre for Medicines Research International Report, CMR 95-66R, November 1995.

Poste G (1994). Presentation to Stock Analysts. London, 12 December 1994.

# 2 Current regulatory reforms and improvements in the review process

FERNAND SAUER

**Summary**

1. In a global market, regulatory agencies cannot remain in isolation; they are judged by companies and the public alike. For comparisons to be valid it is important to know on what basis they are made and to understand that agencies operate within very different frameworks.

2. As a newcomer the European Agency for the Evaluation of Medicinal Products (EMEA) has been in a competitive situation, needing to attract business. Throughout the establishment and operation of the new regulatory system in Europe, the EMEA has monitored its activities and shared its views with industry.

3. Adherence to strict time limits has been one of the quantitative measures of success of the Agency. This has been achieved partly through the introduction of a pre-submission phase and clear dialogue with the applicant.

4. Performance indicators for the Agency have been devised and agreed between the management board and the industry; these will be implemented within the secretariat in 1997.

5. To assess qualitative aspects of the regulatory process, a joint EMEA/EFPIA questionnaire will allow companies to express satisfaction with the whole operation and the secretariat to rate the quality of dossiers.

## Introduction

Many pharmaceutical companies have introduced performance indicators and the regulatory agencies, to some extent, are now doing likewise. Much can and has been learnt from the industry as an agency's task is a mirror image of that performed by a company. Industry collects the data, compiles them in an understandable form and identifies claims, while the agencies, having received these data, disentangle the information and re-evaluate the data, albeit in a shorter time-frame.

Once the EMEA (European Agency for the Evaluation of Medicinal Products) had established its regulatory framework, rather than being the end of a story it was the beginning of a new adventure. For in a global market agencies cannot remain in splendid isolation. In the same way that companies judge each others' performance so, whether they like it or not, agencies are judged by both companies and the public. If this is going to happen it is important to know on what basis comparisons are made, whether they are fair and what can be learnt from the outcome. Hence, there is a need for performance indicators.

## Comparing agencies

When comparing agencies in a global market, it is essential to appreciate that they operate in very different frameworks. Even if the focus is restricted to OECD (Organization for Economic Cooperation and Development) countries, which seem to share the same basic principles for evaluation, the decision-making process might be totally different. Given these different backgrounds, an understanding of where each process fits into the organisation and, indeed, the nature of that organisation, is vital for any valid comparison.

The situation is dynamic. Since all are proud of their regulatory systems there is a sense of challenge with reforms and improvements being made and publicised. It is therefore to everyone's benefit to start with the interests of the patient and ensure a quality review in all parts of the world.

## EMEA

As a newcomer to the regulatory arena, the EMEA was in an unusually competitive situation, for in order to acquire business, it had to devise a regulatory review process that was attractive to industry. The philosophy was to establish and operate a regulatory system and, while so doing, to analyse it, to understand how to do it better and, most particularly, to share these views with industry. The EMEA is convinced that there is a need for partnership with industry and is willing to create this partnership while at the same time it has had to create partnerships with all 15 of the national agencies in Europe.

The EMEA has two core tasks. The first, a new one, is the provision of scientific advice to companies and the second is evaluation of the Centralised Procedure. The additional task of arbitration in the so-called decentralised, or Mutual Recognition, procedure should, it is hoped, only be required occasionally. Finally, the EMEA fulfils activities which require a strong co-ordinating role with the national authorities, like collecting post-marketing data and the co-ordination of Member States' inspections. Although this is a rather complex set of tasks, it is well defined by legislation.

Equally complex is the myriad of partnerships that the EMEA must maintain (Figure 2.1). In order to keep this system together the EMEA organises hundreds of meetings each year and is establishing an internal network or 'intranet'. From the end of January 1997 it will potentially be possible for all concerned to communicate electronically via e-mail, in a structured way, but inevitably it will be some time before optimum use is obtained from this system.

The great diversity of cultures and peoples in the EC further adds to the complexity because different cultures and even different medical practices must be respected. Rather than viewing this as an obstacle, the EMEA regards it as a challenge and the diversity as a source of training and improvement *per se*.

The EMEA's target budget for 1997 is US$32–33 million (28 million ECU) and this is expected to plateau at around

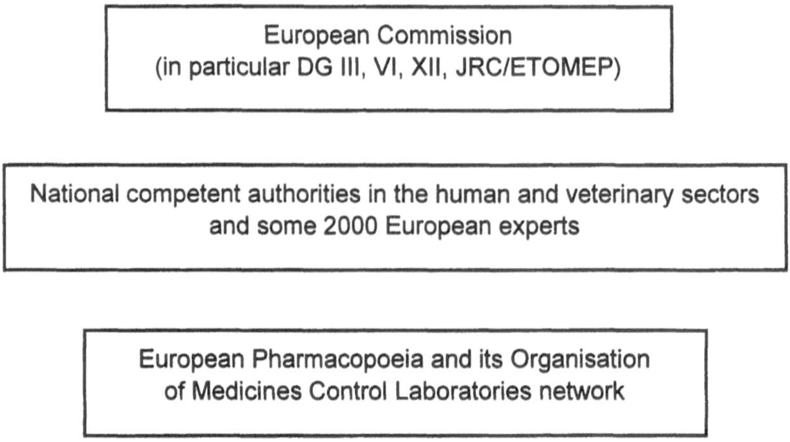

```
┌─────────────────────────────────────────────┐
│          European Commission                  │
│   (in particular DG III, VI, XII, JRC/ETOMEP) │
└─────────────────────────────────────────────┘


┌─────────────────────────────────────────────────────────┐
│  National competent authorities in the human and          │
│  veterinary sectors and some 2000 European experts        │
└─────────────────────────────────────────────────────────┘


┌─────────────────────────────────────────────────┐
│   European Pharmacopoeia and its Organisation     │
│   of Medicines Control Laboratories network       │
└─────────────────────────────────────────────────┘
```

**Figure 2.1** EMEA partners in the European authorisation system

US$55 million by the year 2000. As the old fee structure has proved inadequate, a review is currently under way so that the EMEA no longer has to rely on subsidies but may also receive fees for service. The objective is for 75% of the EMEA's income to be derived from fees by the end of the decade.

**Time-frames**

Adherence to strict time limits, together with the provision of sound scientific advice, are fundamental to the success of the EMEA. In order to meet the relatively short time-frames within the European review procedures, of 210 days for the evaluation of a marketing application and approximately 300 days in total for the whole decision-making process, the EMEA instituted a pre-submission phase of dialogue with the applicant, and this appears to be working reasonably well. Its purpose is to allow identification of any issues that might form a bottle-neck once the regulatory 'clock' has been started, such as legal status of prescription, difficulties with trade names, potential problems with foreign inspections, orphan drugs and so forth.

Keeping to the prescribed time-frames has not been easy. It took over a year to make sure that the initial assessments by rapporteur and co-rapporteur Member States would be communicated to the applicant as well as to other members of the CPMP (Committee for Proprietary Medicinal Products) within the required 70 days. Many national authorities initially considered such a target to be unachievable; however, it can indeed be achieved and it does not undermine the quality of the initial review.

Between days 70 and 120 the other members of the CPMP have the opportunity to review the assessment reports and to raise queries. In this phase there is an open dialogue between authorities and companies; the clock is stopped when the company agrees that it has to provide further information. There follows a very delicate phase linked to the multicultural situation where the opinion and its annexes must be translated into the 11 official languages. Finally, there is a distinct phase, not always obvious in national authorities, of decision making. This 90-day period could theoretically be abolished in an attempt to reduce overall review times; however, it is perfectly legitimate for a new system to provide this time as an extra guarantee.

The challenge to the EMEA has been to make this system work and the achievements for the first 2 years of operation are shown in Table 2.1.

### Performance indicators

The procedures for adopting performance indicators within the EMEA (Table 2.2) started with formal consultations with the industry and culminated in endorsement of those performance indicators by the management board of the Agency in December 1996. This initiative was accompanied by cost surveys and time recordings, in an attempt to make the quantitative components more visible.

The main element of the action plan for introducing performance indicators is the publication of decision tables (Table 2.3), underpinned by the introduction of an application tracking system

17

**Table 2.1 Results (December 1996)**

CPMP:

38 positive central opinions

3 pharmacovigilance opinions

25 scientific advices

CVMP:

2 positive central opinions

253 maximum residue limits (MRLs)

Commission:

28 European marketing authorisations

**Table 2.2 EMEA performance indicators: Procedures**

- Outcome of wide consultation with industry

- Discussed and endorsed by management board

- Implementation in 1997 within EMEA secretariat

- Cost surveys and time recording

- Extension in 1998 to EMEA scientific parties

(ATS) which is now the subject of training. It could be generalised throughout the Agency by June 1997. By the end of the year it should be accessible to all members of the CPMP and maybe in another year's time it will allow companies a window on the tracking of their application.

## Quality

The quantitative aspects of the regulatory process are easily made public but the quality aspect is the most delicate and one for which there is no solution at present. External audits are conducted and

**Table 2.3  EMEA performance indicators: Action plan**

- Monthly publication of decision tables and timing

- Phasing in of ATS (electronic tracking)

- EPARs/MRLs on the Internet

- Joint EMEA/EFPIA questionnaire

- Quality management system

since evaluation reports are available on the Internet they are open to scrutiny by the scientific community. However, this is not enough, so the EMEA, in conjunction with the EFPIA (European Federation of Pharmaceutical Industries' Associations), has recently finalised a questionnaire specific to each product. This will allow companies to express their degree of satisfaction with the quality of the whole operation and allow the EMEA secretariat to rate the quality of the dossier. The results will be analysed by a joint EFPIA/EMEA panel and it is hoped that the issues raised by the survey will be scrutinised maybe two or three times a year in a joint session between the CPMP and representatives from the EFPIA. The whole system is being underpinned by a quality management system within the secretariat to consolidate what has been achieved already.

The EMEA considers that it is co-responsible with the European Commission for the full decision-making process. It is not sufficient to show that the EMEA has performed according to its standards; these have to lead to a tangible result for the patient.

# 3 Current regulatory reforms: CBER

KATHRYN ZOON

**Summary**

1.  To achieve the strategic objective of managing the review process from discovery through to post-marketing surveillance, the Center for Biologics Evaluation and Research (CBER) has established a managed review process project. The aims of this project are to identify existing obstacles to managed review, to design new business processes and improve existing or eliminate redundant processes.

2.  To this end, a number of core teams have been gathering and analysing information. The Center's business processes have been mapped in great detail and first line recommendations are now being considered by the Managed Review Committee before a transition plan is developed and implemented.

3.  A quality assurance unit was established in 1996 to monitor the managed review process and determine its effectiveness. This unit also serves the function of ombudsman for dispute resolution, ensuring fairness and consistent policy application.

4.  The unit has primary responsibility for auditing the review process. Quality measurements of importance are identified and routine programme evaluations conducted. In addition, oversight meetings are held to scrutinise the reasoning behind 'clinical hold' and 'refuse to file' decisions. These meetings have proved useful, not only in reversing some of the decisions but also as a staff training exercise.

**Managed review process project**

Management of the review process itself was one element of the Prescription Drug User Fee Act (PDUFA: 1992) that challenged both CBER (Center for Biologics Evaluation and Research) and CDER (Center for Drug Evaluation and Research). CBER has a particularly broad mandate to manage, since it is responsible not only for therapeutics, vaccines and traditional blood products but also for allergenic products, tissues, cellular and gene therapies, biological diagnostics and for screening the safety of the blood supply, including responsibility for HIV-related issues. To meet the PDUFA goals there was a need to manage the process from the end of Phase II through review of the application. This project was successfully implemented in November 1993 at CBER, not only for PDUFA products but for all CBER products.

As one of the goals of CBER's strategic planning initiative instituted in 1995 was to manage the review process in a seamless way from the point at which CBER first interacts with a new product through post-marketing. The managed review process project includes several steps, one of which was to outline and re-invent a number of the organisational business processes.

To accomplish this large task a number of roles and responsibilities were defined (Figure 3.1). A managed review committee was established and several core teams set up to examine the Center's business processes; these teams were comprised of CBER staff, such as reviewers and first line managers, aided by outside facilitators.

*Scope*

The Center extended the PDUFA requirement for a managed review process to include pre-IND, IND (investigational new drug) and post-marketing surveillance activities. All relevant activities, milestones and benchmarks were examined; obstacles to a managed review process were identified and solutions found by focusing on:

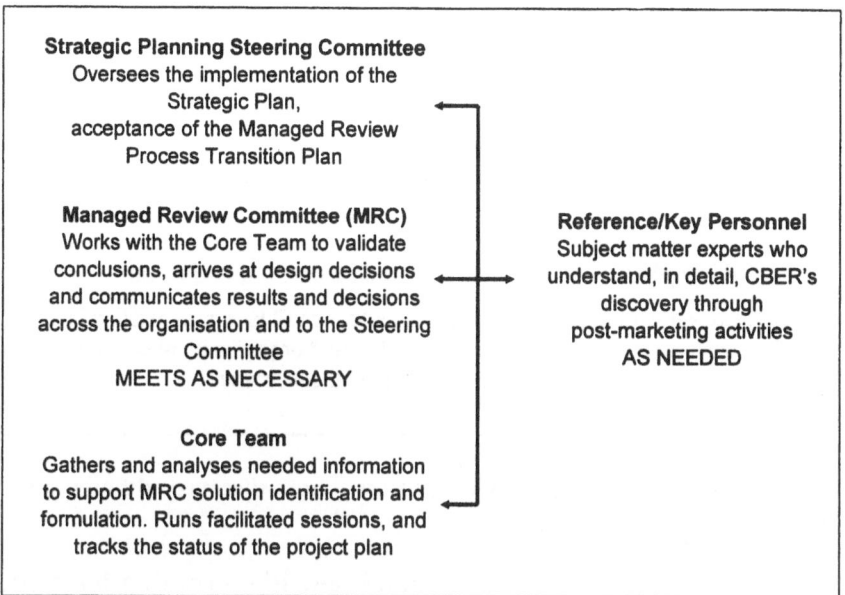

**Figure 3.1** Managed review process project – structure/roles and responsibilities

*process and information flow*: part of mapping the business systems;

*information systems and technology interaction*: business processes were reviewed, mapped and re-structured before IT systems were overlaid;

*organisational roles and responsibilities*: delegation to the lowest possible level with people empowered to make decisions and be held accountable for them;

*personnel skill requirements*: to intertwine expertise (not everyone needs a PhD or MD) for various tasks and maximise personnel efficiency.

In addition, relationships outside CBER that would be affected by the managed review process were identified and analysed.

The objectives of the managed review process project are summarised in Figure 3.2. Many of these are not one-time activities because once a process is in place and evaluated there are always

---

**Objectives**

- Identify existing obstacles and issues

- Design new processes

- Improve existing processes

- Eliminate redundant processes

- Eliminate processes that provide little or no added value

CBER's re-engineered managed review process will leverage existing information systems, technology, personnel, skill, and organisational structure as well as establish requirements for changes in these areas.

---

**Figure 3.2** CBER's managed review process – from discovery through post-marketing surveillance

new ways to look at the business and new ideas coming forward. So periodic reviews of business processes are being developed within the organisation to allow new techniques to be implemented in the future.

*Mapping activities and current status*

In order to map any one of the Center's processes, each unit of work activity was identified and the various elements under that activity defined. Each of these elements in turn were mapped likewise. Since CBER has an extensive series of business processes that relate to its activities from pre-IND to post-marketing the total map is vast; a higher level analysis is shown in Figure 3.3.

These mapping activities are now complete and first line recommendations by the core teams are being considered by the Managed Review Committee. Specific suggestions will be taken to the strategic plan leaders and a transition plan implemented to facilitate passage to the new system.

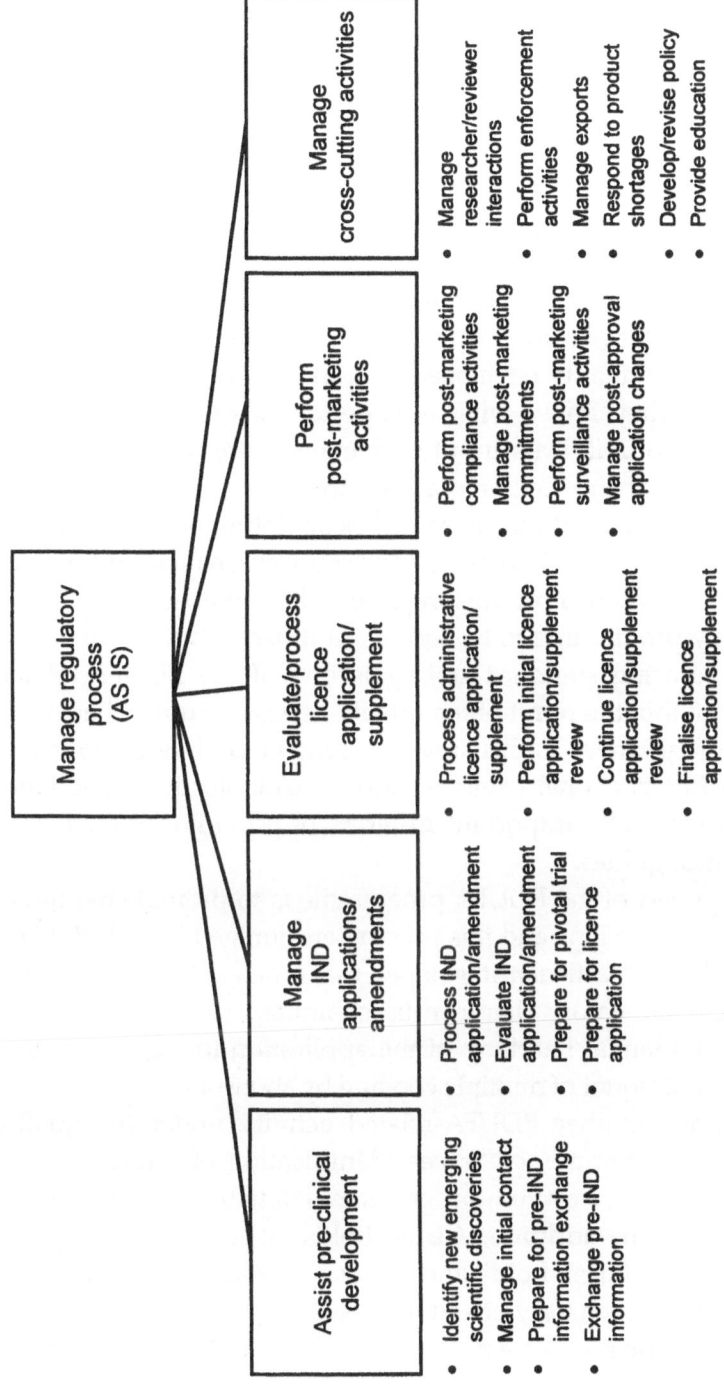

**Figure 3.3** Mapping of the Center's business processes

## Quality assurance programme

A quality assurance unit was established in 1996 to monitor CBER's managed review process. Among its multiple functions is the role of ombudsman, looking at dispute resolution, fairness, intercentre jurisdiction and policy applications. For example, random audit checks of letters to industry are made to ensure consistency with the agency's policies.

The programme has been used in a number of the managed review processes (Figure 3.4) including the actual implementation. Two aspects of quality have been built-in from the beginning. Staff are trained; they know what is expected of them and are held accountable to that. Data input and analysis are reviewed so that the activities of the Center are monitored and timeliness maintained. At the same time there are clear definitions of roles and responsibilities so that there is consistent co-ordination between units in cases where a product might overlap groups.

For any programme to be successful it has to have clear standards. Monitoring standard setting is one of the PDUFA-related activities within the remit of the quality assurance unit. There are a number of initiatives in this area including Good Review Practices and ICH (International Conference on Harmonisation). The latter has been especially important in terms of providing higher level performance guides.

A large part of the PDUFA programme is to promote the use of electronic submissions and this is being encouraged by CBER wherever possible. In particular it is hoped that much of the line listing of patient and laboratory data can be submitted on CD ROMs; this will reduce manual handling of the application for regulators and decrease the amount of multiple copying by sponsors.

Auditing, another PDUFA-related activity under the quality assurance programme, embraces identification of critical quality measurements and routine programme evaluations, both internal and external. In addition, CBER holds oversight meetings to review 'IND clinical hold' and 'refuse to file' decisions. These meetings have been very effective in reducing the number of both types of decision and have proved useful as staff training exercises,

---

**Managed Review Process (MRP)**

- Implementation of the 'to be' MRP
- Quality and consistent review activities
- Responsible data collection
  - FDA review standards
  - clinical drug development practices
- Clear definition of roles and responsiblities
  - authority
  - accountability

---

**Figure 3.4** CBER's quality assurance programme

emphasising that there must be legitimate reasons before these decisions can be made.

### Re-inventing Government initiatives

The impact of several of the REGO II (Re-inventing Government) initiatives (Zoon, 1996) is now apparent. The Phase II rule to reduce the need for reporting certain manufacturing changes for biologics, issued in January 1996, is expected to decrease the number of submissions by 50%. The final rule was published in July 1997. This represents a significant public health improvement as changes and new technologies will be implemented faster and lead to better products.

One of the most significant changes has been the elimination of the requirement for an Establishment Licence Application (ELA) for specified biotechnology products such as monoclonal antibodies, recombinant DNA-derived products and certain other therapeutic factors. This rule was published in May 1996. Lot release for specified biotechnology products was also eliminated, in late 1995.

One of the major initiatives, jointly with CDER, has been the development of a harmonised application form. This is a first step towards the ICH goal of a global dossier.

Since not all biologics were affected by the elimination of the ELA, a single application, called the Biological Licence Application, is now being developed for all biologics. The information on the chemistry, manufacture and control of products as well as information on establishments for products other than specified biotech products, will be laid out in the format of the guidance documents for the harmonised application. Additional guidance is available for non-clinical laboratory and clinical studies. The overall requirements for all applications will be reduced in terms of the necessary information.

## Conclusions

The re-invention of CBER's regulatory framework and business processes has been a unique opportunity to optimise the regulation of biological products. Major progress has been made in our re-invention initiatives for biotechnology and other biological products. CBER's strategic plan for 2004, in particular the managed review process from discovery through post-marketing, is on track and will have a major impact on making safe and effective biological products available to the public as rapidly as possible.

## Reference

Zoon K (1996). What strategies should be considered for implementation by the end of the century? CBER vision. In: Lumley CE, Walker SR (eds.), *Improving the Regulatory Review Process: Industry and Regulatory Initiatives*, Kluwer Academic Publishers, Dordrecht, pp. 155–162.

# 4 Improving the review process: The view of the Japanese MHW

YOSHINOBU HIRAYAMA

**Summary**

1. Reform is under way in all stages of the drug approval process in Japan. Following a 2-year review, the Ministry of Health and Welfare (MHW) has amended the Pharmaceutical Affairs Law and related laws.

2. The reforms will strengthen the MHW's role in protocol review, improve the quality of the review process and increase the collection of data on drug reactions. Restructuring within the MHW takes effect in 1997 and staff will double over the next 3 years.

3. Under the amendments, good clinical practice (GCP) is mandatory for all clinical trials. Phase I protocols will be reviewed within 30 days of submission and advice on all protocols can be provided by the Drug Organization, if required.

4. The Drug Organization will check the standard of licensing approval applications and of Re-examination and Re-evaluation Applications. Review of New Drug Applications will be conducted jointly by the Central Pharmaceutical Affairs Council and the Pharmaceuticals and Medical Devices Evaluation Center, a new research institute under the MHW.

5. Finally, the MHW is now executing a policy of transparency regarding the review process, in line with the Japanese government's move towards freedom of information.

## Introduction

Drastic reforms are currently taking place within the Japanese Ministry of Health and Welfare's (MHW) system for reviewing New Drug Applications (NDAs). Two main factors have fuelled the reform of the regulatory review process. Firstly, in the autumn of 1993, Japan experienced a tragic adverse drug reaction (ADR) incident, with 15 related deaths, caused by the combined use of an anti-viral agent named sorivudine and anti-cancer fluorouracil derivatives. Basically, the combination raised the blood level of the anti-cancer agents, which caused severe side-effects. Since the thalidomide disaster, Japanese people have been concerned about the safety of pharmaceuticals, and this incident boosted public concern even more and gave the MHW a fresh chance to reflect on Japan's system on controlling drugs.

The second reason comes from the well-known HIV infection issue caused by unheated blood products. Although the infection itself took place more than 10 years ago, the Japanese courts only recently settled the case involving the HIV sufferers, the manufacturers of the coagulates, and the MHW. In court, the plaintiffs questioned who was responsible for the delay in the development of heat-treated products. They also questioned the delay in the recall of unheated blood products.

These two incidents triggered public outrage and enhanced the MHW's awareness of the safety of pharmaceutical products; hence reform was initiated.

## The process of reform

The Ministry of Health and Welfare conducted an intensive investigation after the sorivudine case to ascertain what caused the tragedy. The survey showed the existence of problems in each and every stage of the drug approval process, namely in the clinical trials stage, that of the NDA review, and that of post-marketing surveillance.

In October 1994 'The Committee for Drug Safety Ensuring Measures' was established by the MHW under the Director Generals of the Pharmaceutical Affairs Bureau (PAB) and the Health Policy Bureau, to tackle the problem. The committee was chaired by Dr Watura Mori, the former President of Tokyo University, and consisted of 18 experts and critics in the fields of medicine, pharmacy, toxicology, jurisprudence and so forth. The committee spent 2 years in earnest discussions to produce two interim reports and a final one.

The first interim report proposed intervention by the authority on the process of drug development and review utilising especially the Drug Organization. The second interim report proposed the overall reform of the review system and post-marketing surveillance.

The Central Pharmaceutical Affairs Council (CPAC) further reviewed these reports and endorsed their recommendations to the Minister of Health and Welfare. Based on these reports and suggestions, the MHW formulated a bill to amend the Pharmaceutical Affairs Law (PAL) and related laws and laid it before the 'Diet', the Japanese parliament. The bill passed the Diet and was promulgated in June 1996 to go into effect in April 1997.

### Role of the Drug Organization

The Drug Organization is legally authorised by the Minister of Health and Welfare and its role and functions are stipulated in the Law concerning the Organization for Drug ADR Relief, R&D Promotion and Product Review.

Most of its personnel are derived from government offices, mainly the MHW. They usually spend several years in the Organization and then go back to their original offices. All personnel are under legal controls similar to those in government offices. For example, they are under a strict obligation of secrecy concerning information obtained through work, just as government workers are.

The Drug Organization, established in 1979, has an interesting history. Initially it was a fund to provide relief for sufferers from drug reactions; the departments dealing with that function are the oldest in the Organization (Figure 4.1). Then, in 1987, a new

31

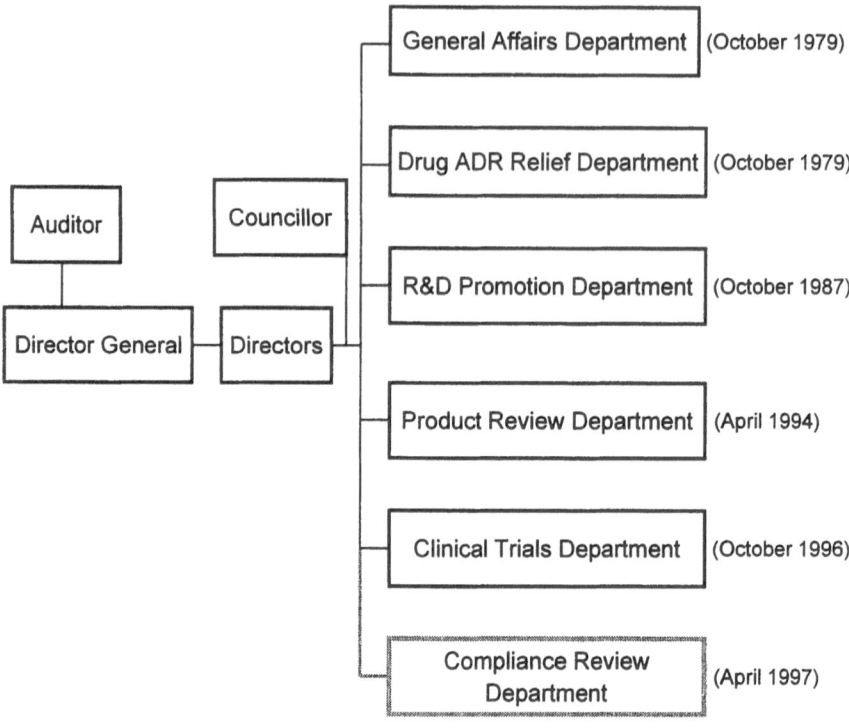

**Figure 4.1** Organisation and history of the Drug Organization

department was added to the structure to deal with the function of R&D promotion. Similarly, in 1994, another function, and hence another department, was added for reviewing some classes of drugs such as generics. Thus the Organization has been supplementing the functions of the Pharmaceutical Affairs Bureau by assuming relevant duties.

The amendment in the PAL and other laws in June last year gave the Organization the authority to give advice to sponsors of clinical trials and to guide sponsors when necessary. The Clinical Trials Department was accordingly established in October 1996. In addition, in fiscal year 1997, a Compliance Review Department is to be created and begin operations.

## Current process for drug review

At the clinical trials stage, there is a legal requirement for the protocols of all trials employing new chemical entities to be submitted to the MHW. That Japan's GCP must be observed when conducting trials is one of the PAB Notifications (Figure 4.2).

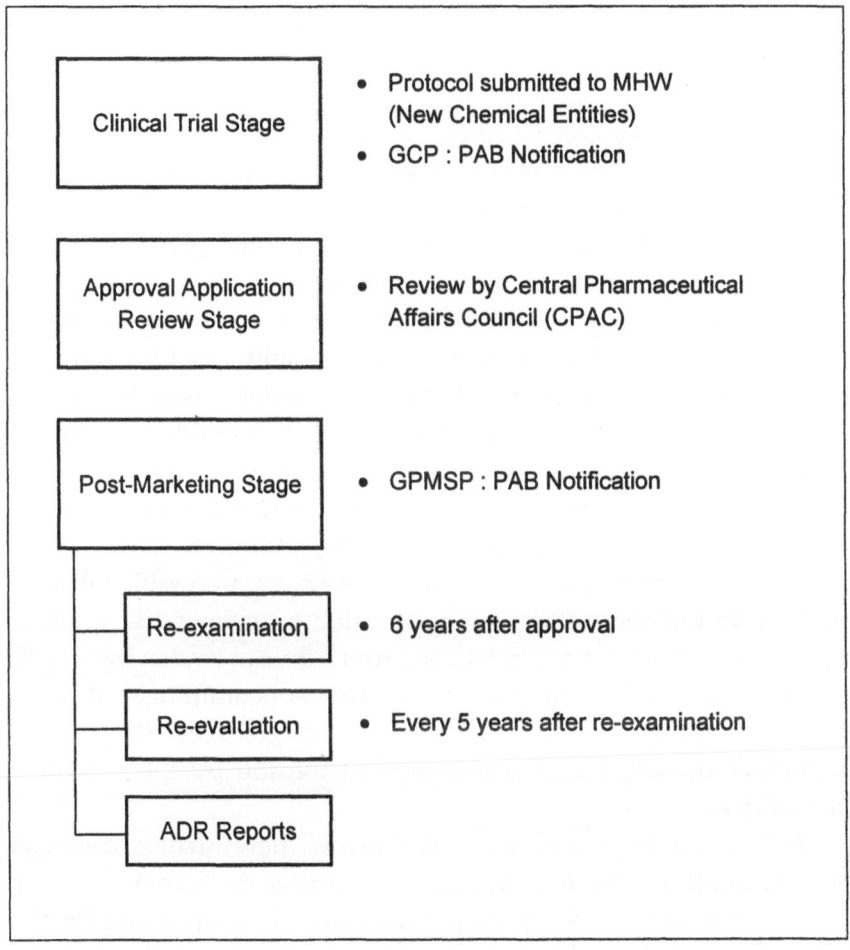

**Figure 4.2** Outline of the current system of the review process

The next stage is the review of the approval applications. A major part of the NDA review is shouldered by the Central Pharmaceutical Affairs Council (CPAC). CPAC consists of three layers, in ascending order: 11 subcommittees in the lowest layer, three committees in the middle layer, and the executive committee on the top; all are involved in the review of new drugs. Each subcommittee deals with drugs in a number of categories. For example, gastrointestinal drugs and endocrinological drugs are reviewed by the first subcommittee. The second subcommittee is responsible for cardiovascular drugs.

Subcommittees consist of experts in medicine, pharmacy, veterinary medicine and statistics, who review a part of the application according to his (or her) speciality. Subcommittees meet once or twice a month; in the process of the discussions, problems about the applications are pointed out and the applicants are required to provide relevant answers to them. The process continues until all the experts in the subcommittee are content with what is presented in the application with respect to the drug's safety and efficacy.

After completion of the review by the subcommittee, the application is presented, with the report by the subcommittee in charge, to one of the three committees. The CPAC committees also consist of experts capable of reviewing NDAs, although more senior scholars tend to be appointed as members compared with subcommittees. In the committee, the application is reviewed in a wider perspective. Committees meet four times a year, reviewing applications that had been passed by the subcommittee at least 2 months before the day the committee meets. New drugs with particular novelty are also reviewed at the top by the executive committee.

Following approval and marketing, new drugs undergo re-examination after 6 years, and are further re-evaluated every 5 years thereafter. This process is intended to compensate for the usually limited size of the clinical trials conducted before approval, and to accommodate information and experience obtained through wider use of the drugs in medical practice.

34

## Reform of the review process

*Amendments to laws*

The main features of the amendments to the Pharmaceutical Affairs and other laws, which will come into effect in April 1997, are shown in Table 4.1. At the clinical trial stage GCP is legally required, and the MHW requires sponsors and investigators to observe GCP. The Drug Organization reviews all protocols in which the products are intended to be used in humans in Japan for the first time, and the MHW gives instructions to the sponsor, if necessary, within 30 days of the submission. The Drug Organization will advise a sponsor on protocols when the sponsor so demands.

When it comes to the review for approval stage, each sponsor is required to ensure the quality of documents contained within registration approval applications. The Drug Organization then conducts investigations on conformity with the standards concerning data for registration approval applications.

**Table 4.1 Outline of amendments of the Pharmaceutical Affairs Law and others**

**Clinical Trial Stage**
  1 GCP legally required
  2 Review and instruction on Phase I protocol by the Drug Organization and MHW within 30 days of submission
  3 Advice by the Drug Organization on protocols

**Review for Approval Stage**
  4 Securing the quality of documents attached to registration approval applications
  5 Investigations on conformity by the Drug Organization

**Post-Marketing Stage**
  6 GPMSP legally required
  7 Securing the quality of documents for Re-examination and Re-evaluation Applications
  8 Investigations on conformity by the Drug Organization
  9 Adverse drug reaction (ADR) reporting legally required

35

Lastly, at the post-marketing stage there is a legal requirement for good post-marketing surveillance practice (GPMSP) the same as in the case of GCP. In addition, sponsors are required to ensure the quality of documents submitted for Re-examination and Re-evaluation Applications. The Drug Organization conducts investigations on conformity with the standards concerning data for Re-examination and Re-evaluation Applications. Finally, the reporting of drug reactions is legally required.

*GCP*

Since GCP is becoming a legal obligation, the present Japanese GCP is being reformulated. Ever since ICH-GCP (which was signed off as a Step 4 document at the International Conference on Harmonisation in May 1996) passed Step 2, the MHW has been consulting with those concerned, including Japan's medical and judicial professionals. A special committee was established within the CPAC and revision has been going on. The revised GCP will be based on ICH-GCP, and shall be promulgated by April 1997, when the amendments of laws go into effect.

*Structural reform*

The current reform aims at strengthening the MHW's intervention, including the review of trial protocols, as well as advice, strengthening the compliance review of data submitted for New Drug Applications, Re-examinations or Re-evaluations, and improving the quality of the review process. It is also aimed at bolstering ADR information gathering and analysis. In order to realise an expansion of duties of this size, the MHW needs a larger staff.

There has therefore been a drastic restructuring within the MHW (Figure 4.3) which includes the following: firstly, new departments have been established in the Drug Organization which will aid the MHW's activities. Secondly, the MHW will divide the functions now handled by the Pharmaceuticals and Cosmetics Division into two. Specifically, the administrative matters concerning drug review will be handled by one section of the MHW. In addition, under the National Institute of Health Sciences,

**Current**                                    **After reform**

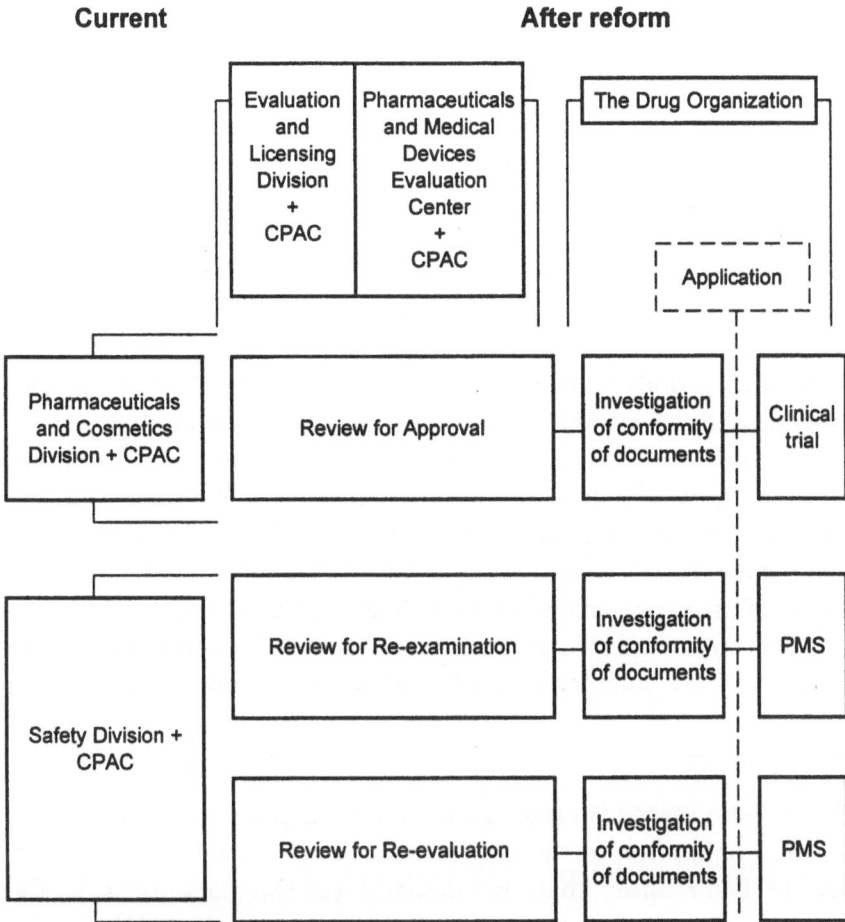

Figure 4.3  Organisational reform of the review process

which is a research institute under the MHW, 'the Pharmaceuticals and Medical Devices Evaluation Center' (the Review Center) will be established to take charge of specialised review. Thus, the duties currently shouldered alone by the MHW or, more specifically, by the Pharmaceuticals and Cosmetics Division, will be jointly carried out by the MHW, the Drug Organization and the Review Center.

Of particular note is that the Review Center will be in charge of some parts of the NDA review. As previously mentioned, NDA review has been conducted solely by the CPAC. After the reform, however, the Review Center, which is part of the MHW, employing technical officials with expertise in medicine, pharmacy and other scientific fields, will jointly review the applications with the CPAC. It is planned that in order to accumulate experience in NDA review, technical officials in the Review Center should remain in their posts longer than is usual for other MHW officials, who are generally transferred every 2–3 years.

Currently, the responsibilities for drug review are allotted to two divisions in the MHW according to the life-cycle of a drug. One division is in charge of matters before approval, the other division bears the responsibility for matters after approval. Under the new system, obligations will be allotted according to the similarity of the tasks. Thus, the Drug Organization will take charge of examining the reliability of data submitted for New Drug Applications, Re-examinations and Re-evaluations. The Review Center will conduct the review in conjunction with the CPAC. The MHW will supervise the administrative procedures for giving approval, and so forth.

This structural reform takes effect in 1997 but, in terms of size of the staff, it is planned that this will double in about 3 years.

### Transparency

So far, little information on the drug review process has been open to the public, due to the requirements of secrecy. Now, however, the MHW realises that the demand on the patients' side for information on pharmaceuticals has increased tremendously. In particular, informed consent is becoming the norm in the Japanese medical scene, and this requires doctors to give information to patients. Moreover, the Japanese government is generally moving towards freedom of information.

In such a context, and taking into account the argument that more information should have been given in the HIV infection issue, the MHW has been executing a policy of transparency concerning the content of relevant CPAC discussions after the drug is approved. In principle, reports and minutes concerning the review process are prepared by the CPAC and the MHW and, taking trade secrets into consideration, are then disclosed to the public.

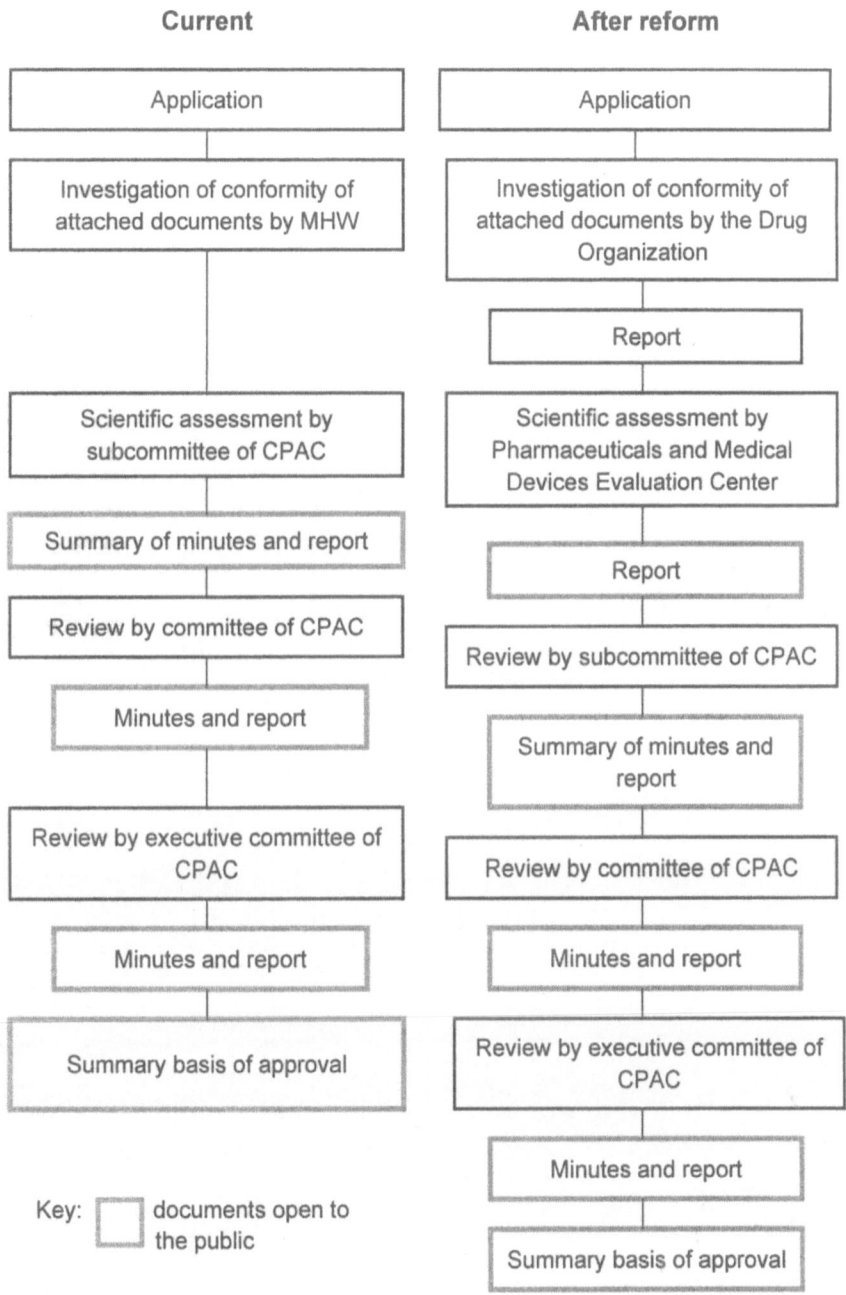

**Figure 4.4** Transparency of the new drug review process

For new drugs approved after October 1996, the CPAC report on the drug, the minutes of relevant CPAC meetings (subcommittee, committee and executive committee) and a list of documents submitted for the approval application have been available to the public (Figure 4.4). In addition, after the reform, the review report formulated at the Review Center will also be made public.

# 5   Comparing the performance of the Canadian TPD with other regulatory authorities

BETH PIETERSON

---

**Summary**

1.  A study, commenced in 1995, by the Canadian Therapeutic Products Directorate (TPD), to ascertain and compare published statistics for 'internationally competitive' performance targets for the regulatory review process, revealed differing philosophies in the setting of targets. Whereas some major regulatory agencies provided targets for each step of the review process, others solely addressed the assessment part of the review.

2.  The published target times for the complete review/assessment of submissions on new active substances varied from 301 calendar days in the UK to 545 calendar days in the USA. Actual performance by the agencies (Australia, Canada, Sweden, the UK and the USA) also varied.

3.  More important than the figures, however, was the finding that the study promoted an understanding of the terminology and processes used in the different agencies. Without such understanding, meaningful comparisons cannot be made.

4.  In general, more information is being communicated to industry on regulatory performance. Most agencies are using, to some extent, the same set of methods to improve the submission review process.

## Background

The Canadian Therapeutic Products Directorate published its first performance targets in 1994 but, prior to this, significant changes were being made in its approach to managing the review process. In the first version of the 'Management of Drug Submission Policy', published in 1993, the steps in the review process were defined and an electronic tracking system developed to record those steps and measure performance. Since that time the targets have been reduced and redefined, several versions of the management policy have been published and the tracking system changed accordingly. Also, the Directorate's efficiency has improved and approval times have been reduced significantly.

The responses from the industry to the first performance targets were mixed. Although the concept of targets was welcomed there was concern as to whether these targets could ever be met and, more importantly, whether they were internationally competitive. There had not been any scientific/systematic review of other targets before the Canadian ones were published.

*Internationally competitive performance*

During consultations with the industry in 1995, the Therapeutic Products Directorate made a commitment to determine the levels of 'internationally competitive' performance targets and, if necessary, to adjust those in Canada after the exercise. Both sides were agreed that they were unclear what the published performance targets from other agencies actually measured. For instance, the UK's Medicines Control Agency review targets and assessment times were often used by industry, in meetings with the Drugs Directorate, as the gold standard but the Directorate questioned whether these figures included queue times, company time or time for review of additional information, and so forth.

**Comparison of performance standards**

A study was commenced in the summer of 1995 to compare Canadian review performance standards with those of several other major regulatory authorities. The chosen countries, Australia, Sweden, the United States of America and the United Kingdom, had all introduced performance standards as part of their submission review process, but the standards were at different stages of development. Each country deems it important to have published performance standards as a tool for performance measurement as well as for the promotion of transparency and efficiency. Measurements of performance are important for both the authorities and industry, to be able to determine trends, measure improvements and make decisions on resource allocation.

*Study objectives*

The objectives of the study were to:
- Determine what are the targets and what they measure;
- Compare 'total review' targets;
- Compare actual performance to the targets;
- Compare reporting practices;
- Examine trends in methods/tools used to improve the regulatory process.

The original goal was to obtain this information for three main categories of dossier: new active substances, generics or second entry products, and consumer products. Since, in general, the information on the latter two categories was limited, this paper focuses on findings related to new active substances.

Various sources of data were used, from published reports both in journals and regulatory agency reports, to direct communications with industry representatives and the agencies themselves. Lastly, comments of regulators on the draft document were most useful in filling gaps and validating, or disputing, the estimates used in the study when no 'real' numbers could be found.

## Study findings

*Performance targets*

The steps in the review process that are actually measured by the targets in each country are shown in Table 5.1. Both Canada and the USA have published targets for each step in the entire process. The Canadian targets are considered as interim and are not, as yet, in the regulations. The UK's published review standards are for the assessment part of the review process only, from the receipt of a valid submission by the assessor, to completion of the assessment report. In Australia the published review standards refer to the first review only, from receipt of the submission to the decision letter to the sponsor. Sweden publishes review standards for the first review only, from receipt to completion of the assessment report.

Table 5.1  **What do the targets measure?**

|  | Canada | USA | UK | Australia | Sweden |
|---|:---:|:---:|:---:|:---:|:---:|
| Screening | ✓ | ✓ |  | ✓ | ✓ |
| First review assessment | ✓ | ✓ | ✓ | ✓ | ✓ |
| Advisory panel review | ✓ | ✓ |  | ✓ |  |
| First decision | ✓ | ✓ |  | ✓ |  |
| Letter to sponsor (approval/more information) | ✓ | ✓ |  | ✓ |  |
| Screening of response to request for more information | ✓ | ✓ |  |  |  |
| Second review assessment | ✓ | ✓ |  |  |  |
| Final decision to sponsor | ✓ | ✓ |  |  |  |

The lack of performance targets, in some countries, for the whole review process suggests that differing philosophies are used in setting targets.

The target assessment times for the different agencies, given in Table 5.2, show the target for each step (left hand number) and the cumulative number of days for the review process up to that point. All times are shown in calendar days; to convert from working days, a factor of 1.48 was used based on weekends and 11 statutory holidays per year.

**Table 5.2  Target assessment times for new active substances (calendar days)**

|  | Canada | USA | UK | Sweden | Australia |
|---|---|---|---|---|---|
| Receipt | 0 | 0 | 0 | 0 | 0 |
| Completion of screening | 45/45 | N/A | N/A | N/A | 59/59 |
| Completion first review/assessment and notify outcome | 300/345 | 365/365 | 163/163 | 240/240 | 377/436 |
| Screening of response to additional data | 45/390 | N/A | N/A | 30/270 | N/A |
| Complete review/assessment of additional data and notify outcome | 150/540 | 180/545 | 138/301 | 60/330 | N/A/436 |

The UK target of 163 calendar days included the then 80 working days (118 calendar days) assessment target and an average of 30 working days (45 calendar days) for the validation period. The Australian target of 377 calendar days was derived from the 200-day evaluation time, 118 days for the Drug Evaluation Committee meeting time and 59 days for the final decision.

The actual performance figures used in the study are given in Figure 5.1. This information is included solely for the purposes of completeness as it is recognised that all the agencies concerned have improved their performance since this study was conducted.

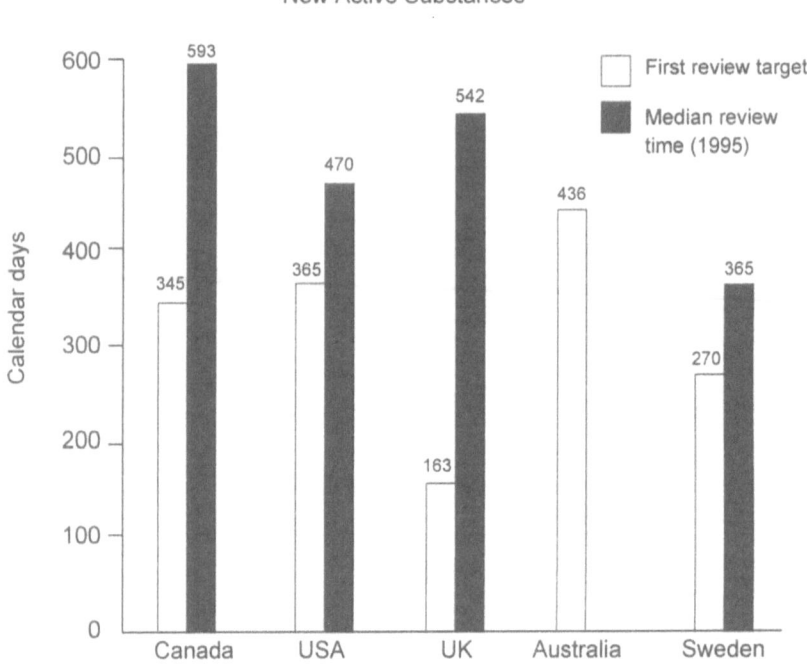

**Figure 5.1** Performance targets and actual performance

*Overall findings*

The findings related to reporting practices can be summarised as follows:

- performance statistics are reported in many ways (for example, percentage meeting the target, averages, medians) and are representative of wide ranges of review times for any given period;
- for any one reporting period it is possible to find a variety of statistics for one agency;
- performance is most frequently reported as submissions approved in a year whereas targets are most frequently applied to the submissions received in a year;
- in general, more information is being communicated to industry on performance by all agencies.

*Methods for improving performance*

The study showed that most agencies were using a common set of tools, to varying degrees, to improve submission review performance. The following trends were noted:

- business-like approach for managing the review process;

- quality management projects;

- increased emphasis on the quality of submissions;

- increased emphasis on screening/validation to ensure complete and high quality submissions;

- increased communication with industry regarding the quality of their submissions, and formal training in some cases;

- team approach to submission review;

- faster responses from industry to requests for more information;

- and faster reviews of that information by agencies.

## Usefulness of the study

From the Directorate perspective, the study was considered useful and it was successful in comparing international targets for new active substances. The study promoted the understanding of terminology and processes used in the different agencies. Without such understanding, meaningful comparisons cannot be made. With today's focus on harmonisation, an understanding of the review processes in other countries is increasingly important.

The Pharmaceutical Manufacturers Association of Canada conducted its own parallel study, using its sources of data and, after some discussion, the two studies arrived at the same final charts. The mutual trust developed through this process made the study useful.

Ideally, review times for the same set of submissions reviewed within the same period would form the best basis for a meaningful international comparison. Several retrospective studies of this nature have been done but the varying rates of organisational and process renewal or change in the agencies, and the varied timing of submission receipt, make these comparisons less than ideal.

## Conclusions

By way of conclusion, I would like to pose some questions related to performance and performance targets for consideration.

- How fast is fast enough; how do we know when we get there?

- Is it time to refocus some of the energy that has been directed, by both the regulator and the regulated, at eliminating some of the backlogs and decreasing approval times into reducing the time of other steps in the drug development process?

- How important is quality? How can the quality aspect of the scientific assessment be measured and communicated to the stakeholders?

# 6  Measuring performance: The view of the TGA

JOHN McEWEN

---

**Summary**

1.  In 1991 the Baume Report made 164 recommendations, all of which have been implemented, for revising the process of drug evaluation in Australia.

2.  In particular, performance standards were set for the Therapeutic Goods Administration (TGA). The three main phases of the drug evaluation procedure, from acceptance of a valid submission to the final decision, must be completed in 255 working days.

3.  Responsibility for meeting the performance standards for new active substances and major variations rests with the heads of four clinical evaluation units within the Drug and Safety Evaluation Branch of the TGA.

4.  For the first 8 months of 1996, all applications were reviewed by the TGA within the target times. However, the total time from submission to registration in Australia was longer than expected, due to protracted sponsor response times.

5.  Among issues for future consideration is the need to review the nature and number of questions asked by the TGA and the delay in reply by sponsors. Also the value of pre-submission and post-evaluation meetings might be explored.

## Introduction

In the early development of drug evaluation in Australia, there were close similarities with the early evolution of evaluation in the United Kingdom, following thalidomide. A capacity to evaluate drugs for efficacy and safety, in addition to quality, was created within the federal Department of Health and an expert advisory committee – the Australian Drug Evaluation Committee (ADEC) – was established. Perhaps because of its independent establishment, unique data requirements, formats and procedures grew up in Australia and this lack of harmonisation with the rest of the world resulted in much discontent within the Australian pharmaceutical industry in the 1980s, leading to several enquiries and reviews.

## Review of drug evaluation

The review with the greatest impact was conducted by Peter Baume, in 1991 (Baume, 1991). Baume was a gastroenterologist and former federal Minister. He made 164 recommendations, all of which were implemented.

Baume recommended that applications in the European Union format be accepted in Australia. No longer would there be unique Australian data format or content requirements. At the same time, he recommended Australia stop developing unique Australian standards for drugs and cease using existing Australian standards for drugs unless there was a demonstrated public health need for an Australian standard.

Baume also recommended performance standards to be met by the Therapeutic Goods Administration (TGA). These performance standards have since been incorporated into the Therapeutic Goods Regulations. For products where there is a need to evaluate toxicological or clinical data – which broadly includes what would be known in the European Union as 'New Active Substances' and 'Major Variations to Existing Marketing Authorisations' – the standard was set by Baume at 255 Agency Working Days. That period spans from acceptance of a valid submission to the final (approve/ not approve) decision.

The Regulations also include the provision that for this type of application the sponsor must pay 75% of the evaluation fee at acceptance of the application. The remaining 25% is payable on the day of notification of the decision at the end of the process but that 25% is not payable if the decision is not notified within the 255 working days. Baume saw this as a means to encourage TGA to meet its target deadlines.

### Australian drug evaluation procedure

The objective of the TGA is to ensure the safety, quality and efficacy of therapeutic goods available in Australia at a standard equal to that of comparable countries and that the pre-marked assessment is conducted within a reasonable time. The flow-chart for the Australian procedure is shown in Figure 6.1. Outside the previously mentioned 255 working days is an initial period in which the application is screened and valid submissions accepted; a maximum of 40 working days is allowed for this process. The subsequent review procedure is divided into three main phases (Figure 6.1):

Evaluation Phase – from acceptance of a valid submission to availability of a written evaluation report on each part of the data;

ADEC Phase – this includes the drafting of a proposed decision and a subsequent period for the sponsor to consider the proposed action and provide written comment for consideration by the Committee;

Decision Phase – a period in which negotiation can occur before the decision is notified.

The figure of 80 Agency Working Days for the ADEC Phase is potentially misleading. It is based on the current practice of ADEC meeting every 2 months and takes into account the proposed

51

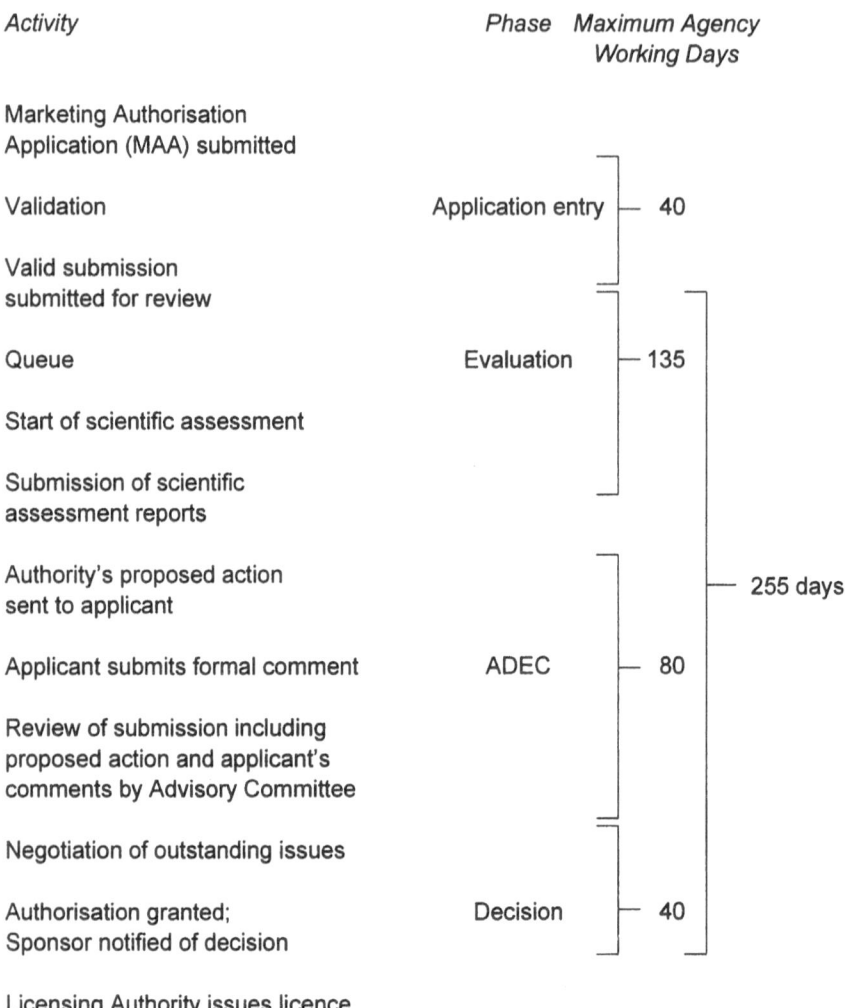

**Figure 6.1** Australian drug evaluation procedure

action being ready on the day after the close of an ADEC agenda. In such a case, the submission would not be considered until the following ADEC meeting almost 4 months later. The ADEC Phase would then take 80 Agency Working Days. In practice, most proposed actions are written just prior to the close-off date and this can contract the ADEC-Phase to about 44 Agency Working Days.

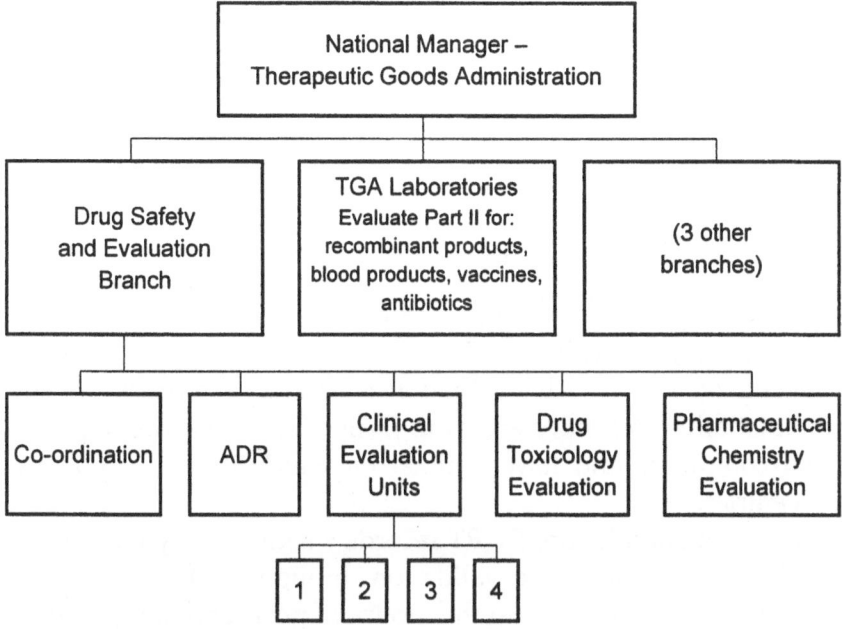

**Figure 6.2** Organisation of the Therapeutic Goods Administration

The additional time could theoretically be used for evaluation, expanding the available evaluation time to about 170 Agency Working Days. In practice, this does not happen often.

The organisation of the Drug Safety and Evaluation Branch of the TGA is shown is Figure 6.2. Also shown are the Therapeutic Goods Administration Laboratories (TGAL) whose staff undertake the Part II evaluations of biotechnology products, blood products, vaccines and antibiotics.

The responsibility for meeting performance standards for assessment of new active substances and major variations rests with the four Clinical Unit Heads, each of whom has responsibility for a number of therapeutic categories. The Clinical Unit Heads are directly responsible for arranging the clinical evaluation and, through the Section Heads of Toxicology Evaluation, Pharmaceutical Chemistry Evaluation and the various TGAL Sections, for the timely evaluation of the Part II and Part III data. The Clinical Unit Heads or their immediate deputies are responsible also for summarising the outcomes of the three parallel evaluations and preparing the proposed action.

The Clinical Unit Heads have the legislated power to make the decision to approve/not approve. They seek the advice of ADEC on their proposed action but are not bound by that advice.

### Monitoring TGA performance

The recording of regulatory performance is supported by a mainframe computer facility – Drug Applications for Registration Tracking or DART. All evaluation staff and a number of key administrative staff have access to DART from their desktop personal computers and have defined responsibilities for updating data entries.

For each submission, DART records a series of key dates from the date of receipt before validation through to the date of the decision and then beyond to the receipt of post-marketing reports. Some information about payment of fees is recorded also. The recording is in quite fine detail and includes dates of commencement of the various parallel evaluations and some specialist evaluations (such as evaluation of sterility by the Microbiology Section), the steps in the ADEC Phase and the steps in the post-ADEC negotiation phase (Decision Phase). At initial entry and later at each data entry, DART calculates various 'due dates' in accordance with the defined performance criteria. There is also provision for recording the actual date of completion of each step. Sponsors are able to have on-line access to information about their applications.

The TGA is entitled to ask questions of the sponsor during the evaluation process. These are called 'Section 31 questions' because the power to seek information comes from Section 31 of the Therapeutic Goods Act. When a question is asked, the performance clock stops until the response is received. The questions and responses are logged on DART and the 'due dates' are amended to take into account the periods for which the clock is stopped.

Currently, DART has only limited analytical facilities. For analyses of performance, data must be down-loaded from DART.

## *Review of performance*

There are several levels at which performance is reviewed. First of all, at the branch level, staff may view information relating to themselves or their workgroup at all times. Within the Branch, the Head, Section Heads and the Senior Administrator receive performance printouts each month and every 8 weeks the Branch and Section Heads meet to review progress of applications and schedule submissions for presentation to ADEC. In addition, the performance of the TGA (including evaluation of prescription drugs) is reported every 3 months to an Industry–Government Consultative Committee which includes representatives of the prescription and non-prescription industries, Department of Industry, Science and Tourism and Department of Finance. Finally, the TGA is a Division of the federal Department of Health and Family Services. As such, the Minister of Health and Family Services is responsible to the Parliament for TGA's performance. TGA's performance is reported to the Parliament each year in the Department's Annual Report.

## Performance levels

In terms of results, the TGA has until recently reported in terms of mean and median values. However, performance data are much more meaningful when reported in terms of percentage of applications completed, as shown in Figure 6.3.

The ambience within the prescription pharmaceutical industry and Government in Australia is generally one of satisfaction with the current performance of TGA in evaluating prescription drugs. However, the total times from submission to registration in Australia – whether quoted in working days or calendar days – are longer than would be expected, given TGA's improved performance. That can be seen in the data presented by CMR International (Thomas *et al.*, 1998) as well as in TGA's own data. The reason for this is that some sponsors are taking a long time to answer TGA questions, as shown in Figure 6.4.

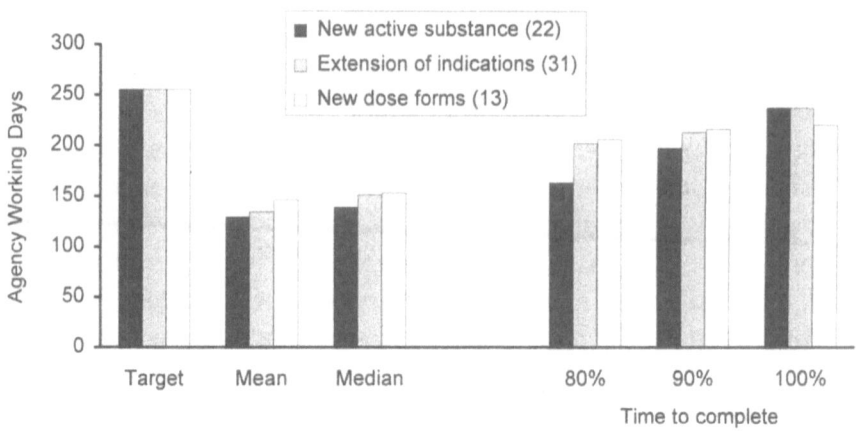

**Figure 6.3** Review times for applications approved (1 January 1996 to 1 September 1996); Agency Working Days

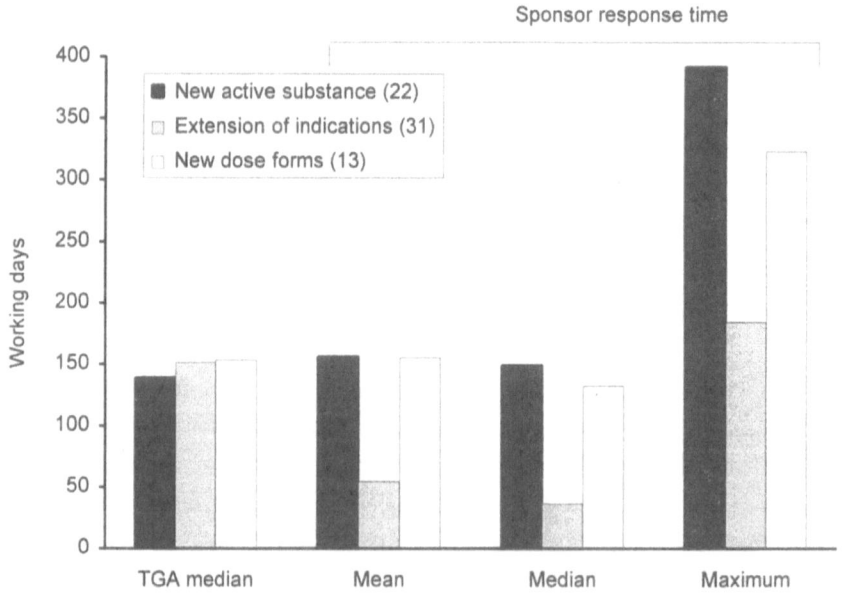

**Figure 6.4** Sponsor response time for applications finalised 1 January 1996 to 1 September 1996

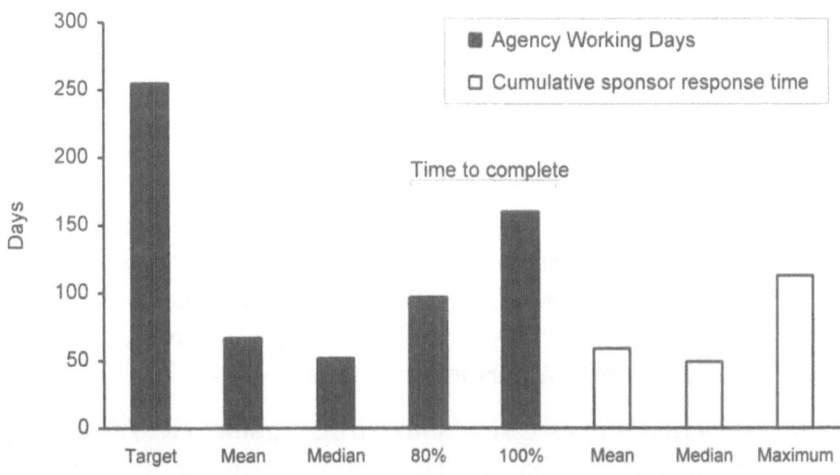

**Figure 6.5** Review times for approval – Five new drugs approved for HIV/AIDS (1 January 1996 to 1 September 1996)

## Issues for consideration

The following presents some of the TGA issues for consideration in Australia, concerning the performance of the TGA.

1.  It would seem sensible for the TGA to report in calendar days, rather than working days. This is likely to be implemented during 1997.

2.  There is a need to review the nature and number of questions asked and the delays in reply by sponsors. Consideration should be given to whether the TGA asks questions not asked by other agencies and, if so, whether such questions are necessary. It should be pointed out that there exists a mechanism by which sponsors can appeal to a Standing Arbitration Committee and receive a rapid ruling on the reasonableness of any question asked during the process. Australian sponsors have almost never used this opportunity for review. Alternatively, is the long time taken by Australian sponsors to provide answers to questions a reflection of the relative unimportance to head office of Australia as a market, or is there another reason?

3. Application entry, prior to acceptance, may sometimes become a long process if further information is regarded as necessary to complete a valid application. This warrants consideration even though it is outside the recorded performance time.

4. Committees such as the CPMP (Committee for Proprietary Medicinal Products) and the UK CSM (Committee on Safety of Medicines) meet more frequently than ADEC. There is a need to consider the impact of having more frequent ADEC meetings on TGA performance times.

5. Experience in assessing some drugs against HIV/AIDS (Figure 6.5) shows that the TGA can perform speedily, with the caveat that some of the data packages were small. It is noteworthy also that the sponsor response times were short. A review of the handling of these drugs may point to more general opportunities for expediting the review process.

6. There is a need to explore the impact of pre-submission and post-evaluation meetings. A small agency, like TGA, has little impact on the development programme of a product. Pre-submission meetings may facilitate the programming of evaluators – personally, I certainly found them useful in reviewing the drugs to treat HIV/AIDS.

7. Two issues of particular importance to a smaller agency are whether:
   (i) TGA can use other agencies' evaluations? Now that Australia accepts applications in the European Union format, applications within Australia are being evaluated earlier and this opportunity therefore seems limited;
   (ii) TGA can enter joint arrangements to share loads by sharing evaluations with other agencies? The impact of this on performance times might be quite complex – it deserves to be studied to ascertain the extent to which the scientific reviews are the rate-limiting step in evaluation.

Finally, on occasions TGA staff obtain assessment reports from other countries and from time to time we do not understand from the report how that agency reached its decision. It is possible that other agencies have made similar comments about TGA reports. This point is raised to stress that it is important that in our endeavours to be timely, the quality of assessment reports must not be sacrificed for speed in review.

## Acknowledgments

I wish to thank CMR International for inviting me to participate on behalf of the TGA. I also wish to thank Dr Malcolm Wright, former head of the Drug Safety and Evaluation Branch, and Mr Andrew Wood, former head of the Branch's Co-ordination Unit for detailed comments on the impact of the Baume report. I wish, too, to thank Dr Susan Alder, the new head of the Branch, for her constructive comments while I was preparing this presentation.

## References

Baume P (1991). A Question of Balance: Report on the Future of Drug Evaluation in Australia. Australian Government Publishing Services, AGPS Press, Canberra.

Thomas KE, McAuslane JAN, Parkinson C, Luscombe DK and Walker SR (1998). A study of trends in pharmaceutical regulatory approval times for 9 major markets in the 1990's. *Drug Information Journal*, **32** (2), May 1998.

# 7 Why have targets for the review process? The view of the EMEA

ROLF BASS

**Summary**

1.  There are five main performance targets applicable to Centralised applications. These include the receipt of high-quality applications, performance of validation, achievement of high-level scientific review, reduction in non-scientific rate-limiting steps and the production by the European Agency for the Evaluation of Medicinal Products (EMEA) of high-quality information.

2.  In support of these targets the EMEA has an ongoing commitment to support and co-ordinate the Committee for Proprietary Medicinal Products (CPMP) activities, to optimise the management of procedures and documents and to encourage the development and implementation of high-standard technical guidance.

3.  To facilitate reaching these targets, an application tracking system is being tested in which the procedure is divided into seven phases, with 28 milestones and 65 actions. The timetable is in line with CPMP meeting dates.

4.  However, it is difficult to see how the target time of 240 days for CPMP opinion plus annexes could be shortened without compromising quality of scientific review (210 days until opinion plus 30 days for transfer of opinion to the European Commission).

5.  Experience since January 1995 shows the average review time until an opinion was given is 170 days; the total review time to a Commission decision is, on average, 380 days (range 155–611 days).

## Background

In considering performance and appropriate targets within the EMEA (European Agency for the Evaluation of Medicinal Products), attention will be focused on the Centralised Procedure for the authorisation of medicinal products in Europe.

For the protection of public health, legislation behind the Centralised Procedure (Council Regulation (EEC) 2309/93) not only ensures the proven quality, safety and efficacy of medicinal products but also emphasises the need for rapid access to those products, where possible. It defines the type of product eligible for the procedure and details the submission process, authorisation, renewal of licences and the need for pharmacovigilance. Information on supervision, sanctions and the tasks to be undertaken are also contained within the regulation.

Rather like a mirror image, the Notice to Applicants (published by the European Commission in July 1997 – Part IIa, and in January 1997 – Part IIb ) reminds the sponsor of the many issues to be taken into account before and at the time of making a submission, as well as during the review period. It describes the need for a consistent regulatory strategy for both the applicant and the authority and details the steps in the procedure from scientific advice to renewal. There is information on the transition from opinion to decision and the means for appeal, if necessary. Finally, the role of the European Public Assessment Report (EPAR) is described.

### Action and interaction

There are a number of major fields in which there is action and interaction involving the EMEA secretariat and the competent authorities within the Member States (Table 7.1). Scientific advice heads this list. A consistent ratio of one scientific advice requested per Centralised application seems to be evolving, although due to the differing time-scales these figures do not apply to the same products: products having been given scientific advice since the middle of 1995, e.g. at clinical development Phases II/III – will be transformed into an application for marketing only later.

**Table 7.1  EMEA targets: Action and interaction**

---

**National competent authorities – EMEA secretariat**

- Scientific advice and other pre-submission issues
- Validation
- Review and assessment report
- Inspection issues
- CPMP opinion
- SmPC, label, leaflet, EPAR
- Post-licensing period

---

Validation is another very important area from the point of view of performance targets. The validation period for an incoming application is 15 days but CPMP (Committee for Proprietary Medicinal Products) meetings are on a monthly basis. To ensure no loss of time, applications have to be received by the EMEA 2 weeks before the next CPMP meeting.

**Proposed targets**

Proposed targets for Centralised applications within the EMEA (and likewise for Member States involved in Mutual Recognition cases) might be condensed into those shown in Table 7.2. The first goal is to achieve high-quality applications every time; when the standard is high then other issues tend to disappear. The validation process should then be performed, not for the purposes of review but to confirm that all that is needed is available and up to standard. Such validation would facilitate immediate scientific review.

These two targets would involve a backward look at the scientific advice period and at the 3–4-month period for regulatory discussions prior to submission. If this period before actual submission has gone well and the application is of a high standard, then validation can provide confirmatory evidence. However,

**Table 7.2  EMEA targets: Centralised applications**

---

- To receive high-quality application
- To perform validation as confirming evidence
- To achieve a high-level scientific review
- Reduce rate-limiting steps
- Produce high-quality information

Mutual Recognition Procedures: Member State targets

---

validation is not that easy to perform and over the period of operation of the EMEA a number of new issues have had to be added to the validation process.

A further objective would be to achieve a high-level scientific review by the rapporteur Member State and the co-rapporteur and their interactions within the CPMP. So that all elapsed time is focused on the scientific review, the next target is to reduce any non-scientific rate-limiting steps. Finally, high-quality information must be supplied by the EMEA once the procedure has been finalised.

## Support by the EMEA secretariat

In order to reinforce these targets the Agency's secretariat is endeavouring to provide a high standard of support and co-ordination to the CPMP. At the same time it is also optimising the management of procedures and documents during the pre- and post-licensing periods through the use of procedural milestones.

There is also support for the development and implementation of high-standard technical guidance in the form of European guidelines (or ICH guidelines translated for use in Europe). This includes the need to train, to facilitate reaching the targets, and to develop and introduce performance indicators (Table 7.3).

To provide a backbone of information for understanding the procedures, a joint EMEA/EFPIA (European Federation of

65

**Table 7.3  EMEA targets: Performance and indicators**

---

- Transparency
    - Table of CPMP opinions
      (identification of rate-limiting steps)
    - Interpretation of interested parties
      (input, information)
- Review criteria
    - Scientific elements (consensus)
    - Timelines (kept)
    - Quality management (AR/EPAR)
    - Benchmarking (EFPIA/EMEA questionnaire)

---

**Table 7.4  EMEA targets: Joint EFPIA/EMEA project**

---

Performance indicators

Review criteria

- Product information
- Milestone dates
- Milestone action
    - Satisfaction (company, co-rapporteur, secretariat)

---

Pharmaceutical Industries' Associations) initiative has resulted in a questionnaire being devised which will be used for all new applications as of 1997 (Table 7.4). It will provide mirror image opportunities for both the applicant on the one side and the CPMP, with rapporteur/co-rapporteur involvement, on the other side to express their degree of contentment or dissatisfaction at different steps throughout the procedure. This initiative will also include a joint evaluation by the EMEA and EFPIA of the results from the questionnaire.

**Table 7.5  EMEA: Centralised Procedure – Phases**

- Phase 1:  Pre-submission
  - scientific questions
  - regulatory affairs questions
  - co-rapporteur
- Phase 2:  Validation of application
- Phase 3:  Pre-review period
- Phase 4:  Review of application
- Phase 5:  Post-opinion phase
- Phase 6:  Decision making
- Phase 7:  Post-authorisation phase
- Phases 4–7  Drug safety/pharmacovigilance

**EMEA quality control**

Internal quality control systems are being developed within the EMEA to cover the management of review/approval procedures, and improved pharmacovigilance and co-ordination of Member States. Standard operating procedures are being prepared to support the interaction between the EMEA parties and applicants.

There is a strong need for a functioning document management system as in 1996 alone the CPMP handled 1100 official documents. These have to be tracked and kept readily accessible in the future. Of particular importance is an application tracking system, which is currently being run as a pilot, and should be in routine use by the end of 1997.

*Application tracking system*

The application tracking system (ATS) currently encompasses seven phases for the Centralised Procedure (Table 7.5), 28 milestones, 65 actions, eight checklists and a variety of template letters. With the tracking system is a control instrument for project management which looks at the timetable according to the type of

**Table 7.6  EMEA: Centralised Procedure: Phase 4 – Review of application**

Milestones

- Day 1:     Timetable (up to 210 days) [11 dates/year]
        – identify problematic issues
        – quality of translations: check
        – need for inspections: check
        – need for working parties/*ad hoc* meetings

- Day 70:    Assessment Reports (rapporteur/co-rapporteur)
        – send to applicant, CPMP, secretariat
        – review, discuss

- Day 120:   List of remaining questions/issues
        – CPMP, first judgement of application
        – send to applicant  –  CLOCK OFF

- Day 121:   Company response  –  CLOCK ON [11 dates/year]
        – need for working parties and/or *ad hoc* meetings
        – Assessment Report (CPMP): draft

- Day 180:   Possibility for oral explanations – CLOCK OFF (opportunity)
        – Assessment Report (CPMP): draft
        – Opinion – SmPC, UPL, labelling: draft

- Day 210:   Opinion – SmPC, UPL, labelling: adopted
        – Assessment Report (CPMP): being finalised

procedure and the application's status at any one time. The status of an application is updated automatically by the tracking system.

Table 7.6 shows the milestones in Phase 4 of the ATS. The timetable is in agreement with the dates for CPMP meetings; 11 are scheduled for 1997 and 12 for 1998. Day 70 is an important milestone as it is the first point at which official information relating to the review process is disseminated in the form of two separate draft assessment reports from the rapporteur and co-rapporteur. This early signalling of what might become a problem is valuable as it frequently enables the applicant to cope quickly with any questions raised.

**Table 7.7  EMEA: Centralised Procedure: Phase 5 – Post-opinion phase**

**Milestones**

- Day 210:  CPMP adopts opinion – SmPC, UPL, labelling
  – Assessment Report being finalised
  – translation finalised:
     company, translation centre, Member States,
     EMEA secretariat

- Day 240:  Opinion plus annexes in 11 languages
     Annex I:     SmPC
     Annex II:    manufacturing author and conditions
                        of the MA
     Annex III:   labelling and UPL
        → Commission
        → Member States
        → applicant
     – European Public Assessment Report (EPAR)
     – EPAR becomes available on the Internet as soon as
        Commission decision is taken

## Review times

The CPMP provides its first judgement of the application at day 120 in the form of an 'approvable' letter which indicates one of three possible outcomes. The first is positive (i.e. likely to be approved); the second is negative (i.e. likely to be refused) and indicates to the applicant that there are serious problems; the third is an in-between variety (i.e. positive outcome possible pending availability of important additional information).

There have been a few examples where the procedure was stopped at this point and an opinion provided. In such cases the total review time is much shorter. For other applications a clock stop of up to 180 days is granted at the discretion of the CPMP to enable the applicant to answer questions, before the application is resubmitted for assessment. Deleting this 'second round' would have a significant impact on total review times.

When using the whole procedure (Table 7.7), it is very difficult to see how the period could be shortened below 240 days as scientific review of applications is not easy and is time-consuming. It is

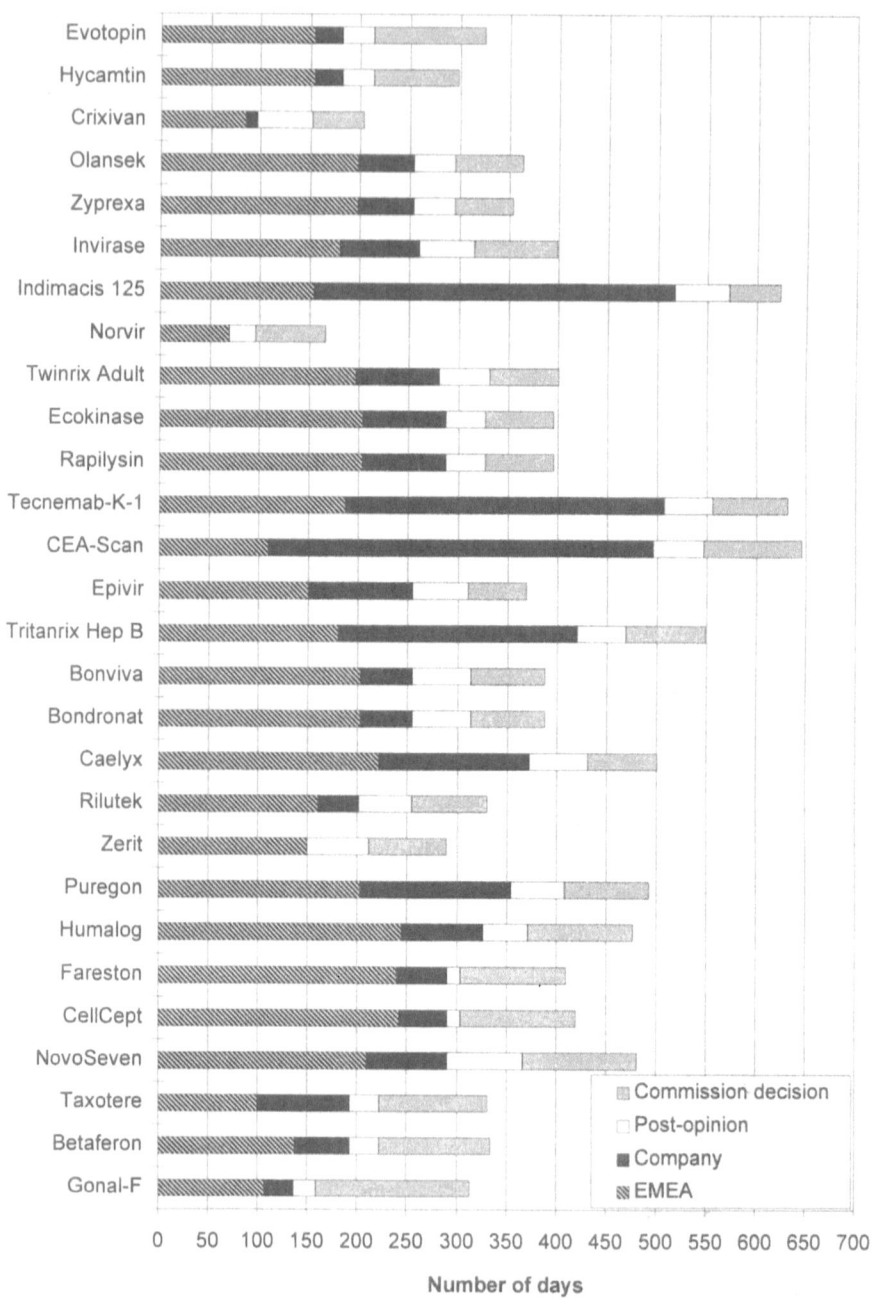

**Figure 7.1** EMEA: Details of timelines for Centralised Procedure products

unlikely that the review would reach the same quality as today if the review time were significantly shortened.

*Recent experience*

Since January 1995, Central applications for 24 new active substances have been given 28 licences by the European Commission. For these, on average:

- Active review time at the EMEA until opinion: 170 days

- Clock stop time: 100 days

- Preparation of opinion (i.e. Agency to Commission): approximately 40 days. Commission decision-making time: 70 days

These figures together add up to 380 days; if the 100 days clock stop is deleted, the average time to complete the procedure is 280 days. As the applications are not the same there is variability: the minimum time was 155 days (no clock stop) and the maximum was 611 days. Details for each application/licence are given in Figure 7.1

It would be interesting to investigate whether the medicinal products with short review times are high-quality products for which a patient need exists. By contrast, maybe longer review times relate to less important products or applications recognised as problematic or of lower quality.

# 8 Why have targets for the review process? An individual viewpoint

EMILY DONNELLY

**Summary**

1.  With the current complexities in Europe, performance targets are essential to drive worldwide competitiveness of the regulatory system. Performance targets provide direction and focus by binding the stakeholders together with a common purpose. These targets should be aligned with the strategic objective and underpinned by performance measures.

2.  There are five main processes in Europe where target setting and performance measurement are vital: provision of scientific advice, Centralised and Mutual Recognition Procedures, post-approval variations and pharmacovigilance. Shorter cycle times are particularly needed for the first four of these processes.

3.  Both the Centralised and the Mutual Recognition Procedures are complex processes with multiple owners that are rate-limiting on the launch of a product. A target of not more than 9 months for the cycle time from submission to launch in 15 markets is proposed for each procedure.

4.  Such challenging stretch goals for both the EU regulatory processes and the parties involved in those processes underline the need for Europe to remain competitive in its approval times.

5.  Agency performances are becoming more directly comparable. Benchmarking information makes the time to availability of new medicines to patients more transparent.

## Introduction

This paper discusses the value of performance targets within the review process and proposes, for consideration by the European authorities, targets for maintaining the competitiveness of Europe in the world market. It presents a personal and biased view of one working in the pharmaceutical industry and focuses on Europe rather than a worldwide approach to targets.

## Targets

### *Why are they useful?*

The simple answer to the question 'why have targets for the review process' is that targets drive performance and the objective is to make performance as efficient as possible. However, in considering performance it is also important to focus on input and output. Performance is largely dependent on the resources put into the process. Adequate resources in terms of skilled individuals and sufficient funding are essential to provide output of satisfactory quality in minimum time.

When setting targets it is important to align them with the strategic objective. In the pyramidal approach (Figure 8.1), the strategic objective might initially be defined as a single mission statement that encompasses the aspirations of all the stakeholders. That will be underpinned by performance targets, normally a small number of concisely expressed 'stretch' goals, that neverthe-

**Figure 8.1** Alignment of performance targets with strategic objectives

less are achievable and can easily be remembered by all concerned in the day-to-day execution of their tasks.

The performance measures supporting these targets are lower level measurements of activities linked to the targets; they are generally rate-limiting in achieving the stretch goals. There are yet further pyramids below for other groups, but before the appropriate infrastructure in target setting can be built, the top pyramid must be perfected. If benchmarking is wanted in the industry, then I believe it is vital that the top pyramid be agreed and made publicly available so that it can be used for benchmarking purposes.

*Strategic objectives*

In setting the strategic objective there is a tremendous opportunity to be inspirational. For example, a group of workers going in each day simply to build an engine might have a different motivation to another group who understand that they are building an engine in order to put a rocket into space. Again, the motivation will be different for a group of workers who believe that they are building a spacecraft to put a man on Venus by the end of the millennium!

In the context of Europe, possible strategic objectives for the authorities could be along the following lines:

> 'to facilitate the availability of medicines of appropriate safety, quality and efficacy as rapidly as is commensurate with the protection and promotion of public health'

or

> 'to establish the best regulatory agency capable of efficiently regulating medicines for 750 million citizens'.

These are just two personal notions; many better alternatives are possible. The point is that, since the system being established in Europe will regulate medicines for a large number of people, it is very important to have a clear strategic objective, understood by all. It is possible that we are in the process of building an agency that will regulate medicines not just for the current 15 EU Member States but also for new Member States from EFTA (European Free

75

Trade Association) countries and maybe some Commonwealth countries too.

The three most important dimensions for setting targets are time, cost and quality. This approach was adopted in discussions between the industry and the European Agency for the Evaluation of Medicinal Products (EMEA) on performance targets, together with the in-built notion of continuous improvement for the Agency, another important aspect of performance.

*Benefits of target setting*

Targets can be used to provide direction and focus for all the parties involved (Table 8.1), both the authorities and the industry, and can bind all the stakeholders together with a common purpose. In my experience, targets also provide motivation and even inspiration to individuals, while offering the opportunity for innovation and process improvement. Finally, target setting and measurement can drive efficient use of resources and continuously improve performance.

**Table 8.1  Targets – benefits**

- Provide direction/focus

- Bind stakeholders with common purpose

- Provide motivation to individuals

- Promote innovation/process improvement

- Promote sharing of best practice

- Promote constructive competition

- Provide sense of achievement

- Drive efficient use of resources

- Drive improved performance

## Performance targets for EU processes

The principal target, and one on which all can agree upon, is the time from submission of an application to launch. In the next two sections some performance targets for Europe are suggested. Although not a comprehensive list, it is hoped that these somewhat provocative proposals will help to move the debate forward.

The five main processes in Europe where performance measurement will be vital include the pre-submission advice to companies during development, the Centralised Procedure and the Mutual Recognition Procedure for obtaining approval, the post-approval variation procedure and activities related to pharmacovigilance (Article 12, Directive 75/319/EEC, as amended).

### *Provision of scientific advice*

The key issue regarding scientific advice is that its provision by the regulatory authorities can be rate-limiting on development time, while within the industry there is pressure to minimise development time. Our need as an industry, therefore, is shorter cycle times for this activity.

In Europe there are two steps that can be rate-limiting. The first is determination of whether the CPMP (Committee for Proprietary Medicinal Products) will be involved in the provision of advice. At present, responsibility for this is split between the CPMP and the EMEA; in due course, responsibility should rest with just one of these groups. The second step is the actual provision of quality written advice; this again comes from collaboration between experts in each organisation.

I contend that for step one, at least 50% of applicants should receive a determination within 15 days; the remainder within 30 days. For step two, the time from submission of the written request to delivery of the written advice, should be no longer than 60 days. These are challenging stretch goals that, although very hard to deliver, indicate the direction in which we should be moving and underline the value of predictable times for these activities.

## Centralised Procedure

From an industry perspective the issues relating to the Centralised Procedure are that the process is rate-limiting on the launch of a product, and it is a complex process with multiple owners (e.g. the EMEA, the Commission, the rapporteur and co-rapporteur Member States).

I propose that the stretch goal for the overall cycle time to launch, including pricing and reimbursement in some countries, might be a maximum of 9 months (Figure 8.2). Within this process, the opinion of the CPMP is needed as quickly as possible and the decision-making process, which combines the activities of the EMEA and the Commission, ought to be faster than the current target of 320 days. Finally, there is a vital need for the EMEA to transmit the appropriate translations from the CPMP to the Commission in a timely fashion so that the Commission can proceed with the decision-making process.

## Mutual Recognition Procedure

The Mutual Recognition Procedure presents the same issues as the Centralised Procedure (Figure 8.2). As these are competitive procedures, I think the target for the cycle time has to be the same. With the objective of filing in the first market and launch in 15 markets this should be no longer than 9 months.

There are three key steps in the Mutual Recognition Procedure that are all rate-limiting. Obtaining national approval in the Reference Member State (RMS) is followed by achievement of mutual recognition. Much progress has been made in achieving both of these steps within the overall target times. The main area where improvement is needed is in the issuance of national licences, which in many cases is longer than 30 days and can be as long as 9 months.

## Variations

The time to approve variations under current procedures is often longer than it used to be under some national processes. In addi-

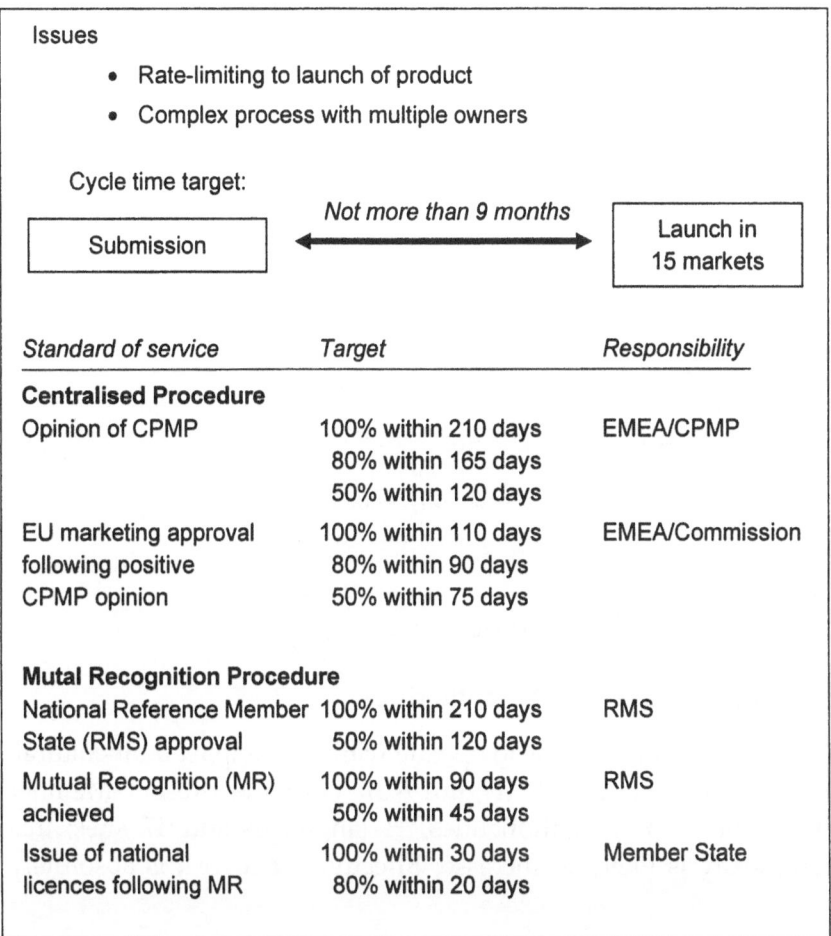

**Figure 8.2** Proposed performance targets – Centralised and Mutual Recognition Procedures

tion, there are some simple variations that might be included in the Type I category, for example pack size. At present there is a decision-making process for Type II variations in the Centralised Procedure that is adding about 100 days to the process. Is this necessary for all Type II variations? It would be helpful to the industry to have a target cycle time for Type II variations of no longer than 90 days for the total process from validated submission to the final decision and for 50% of the decisions to be delivered within 30 days.

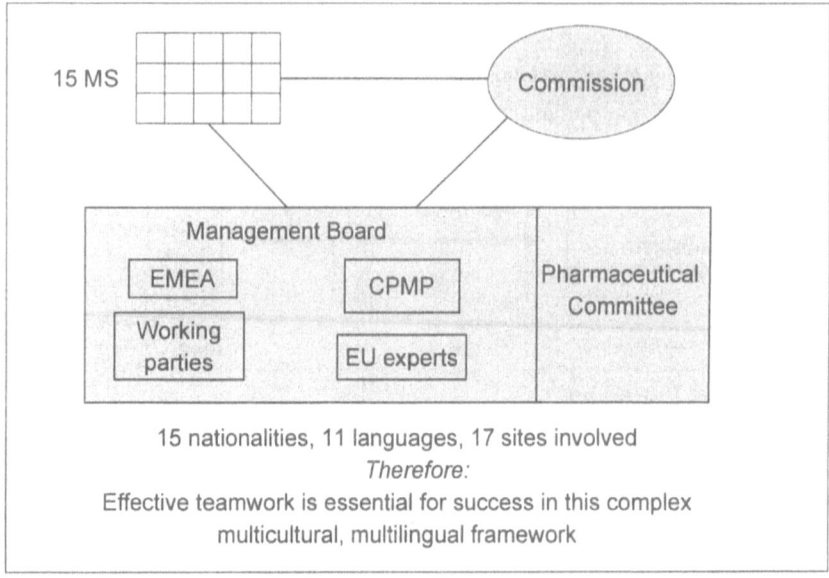

15 MS

Commission

Management Board

EMEA

CPMP

Pharmaceutical Committee

Working parties

EU experts

15 nationalities, 11 languages, 17 sites involved
*Therefore:*
Effective teamwork is essential for success in this complex
multicultural, multilingual framework

**Figure 8.3** New European systems: Key elements

## Performance targets for EU authorities

The system in Europe has to operate within a complex multicultural, multilingual framework (Figure 8.3). With the present Member States there are 15 nationalities, 11 languages and 17 sites; this complexity is likely to increase. Effective teamwork is absolutely difficult when so many people have so many questions, and of information technology literacy in this age of electronic communications.

Above all, the EMEA should be held accountable for the 9-month cycle time from submission to decision; this includes working effectively with the Commission during the decision-making process and being responsible for accurate translations. It also includes effectively working with the Member States, particularly the rapporteur and co-rapporteur Member States during the Centralised Procedure, and the Reference Member State should there be representation during the Mutual Recognition Procedure. Finally, the EMEA should manage approval of Type I variations efficiently.

## The Commission

The industry's hopes for the Commission would be that it provides reasonable legislation, that it be non-bureaucratic in the performance of tasks, professional in approach, resourceful and mindful in the delivery of de-regulation when appropriate.

The Commission currently has responsibility for the delivery of the decision and in my view the cycle time from the CPMP opinion to launch should be no longer than 90 days; in due course, this period should be shortened. Other targets might include a more flexible approach to changing inappropriate or inconsistent legislation, such as that dealing with pharmacovigilance, and a review of decision making for Type II variations.

There are several other groups involved in the EU processes, including the Member States, the CPMP, the Mutual Recognition Facilitation Group, the Management Board and the Pharmaceutical Committee. What are these groups primarily responsible for delivering and what are our hopes in each case? I would urge that a list of targets be prepared for each group so that all may know and understand them.

## Competitiveness of Europe

*Benchmarking agency performance*

The industry is currently developing a global marketplace for pharmaceuticals. In parallel with that, agency performances are becoming more directly comparable because of three initiatives. The first is the harmonisation of regulatory requirements, driven by the ICH (International Conference on Harmonization) process. Secondly, more and more companies are performing simultaneous global development and, lastly, there are more simultaneous global submissions. Therefore, if the start time is the same around the world and the content is the same, the only variable is the time it takes to assess the information.

Benchmarking is now state of the art. Benchmarking agency performance is important as it indicates the comparative speed of access to new drugs for patients and the medical profession. It influences regional attractiveness for R&D, fosters a healthy sense of competition between the agencies and drives process improvements and improved performance.

*Track record*

There has been a considerable degree of improvement in the speed of the regulatory process in Europe in the early part of this decade. The issue of interest to industry is the time taken to launch in 15 markets. Based on our experience at SmithKline Beecham, in 1991 it would have taken 5–6 years to get access to 15 markets (Figure 8.4); by the middle of the decade this figure was just 12 months.

These improvements relate mainly to the Centralised Procedure and the Mutual Recognition Procedure. However, there is also frustration that there is no transparency in availability of information on the Mutual Recognition Procedure and this is an area for improvement.

To exemplify the need for Europe to remain competitive in its approval times, it is worth considering the track record for the first 13 products approved in Europe through the Centralised Procedure. Approval times were faster in the USA than in Europe for 11

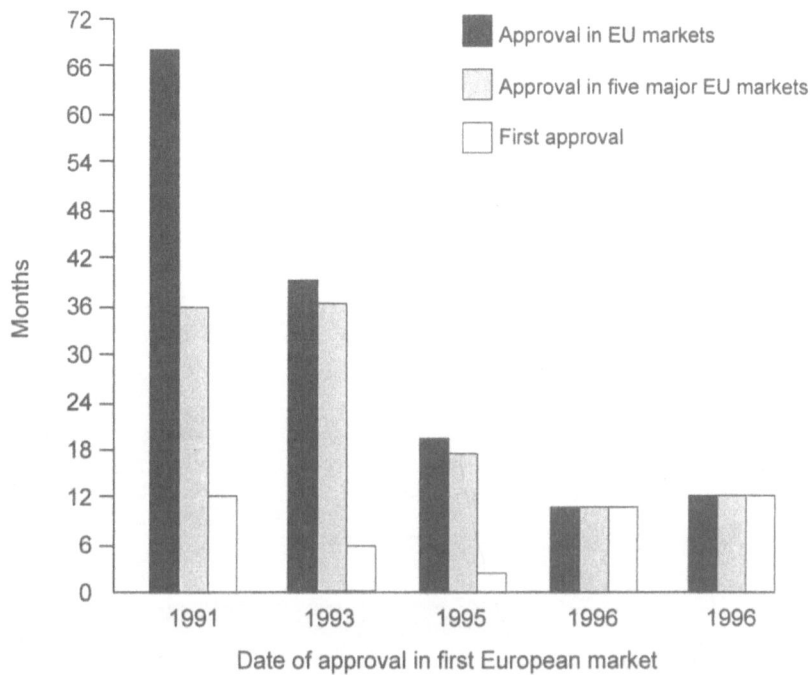

**Figure 8.4** Time to approval for individual compounds in EU markets

of these 13 products (Figure 8.5). It is recognised that this is a biased sample rather than comprehensive data on total performance and that the Food and Drug Administration (FDA) introduced a number of performance improvement initiatives during the last 3 years and is favourably disposed to grant faster approvals for AIDS and oncology medicines

Another way of considering this data is to analyse the year of marketing approval. For this same group of products, ten received marketing approval in the USA earlier than they were technically approved in Europe where, for many countries, there are subsequent steps for pricing and reimbursement prior to launch. This exemplifies the value of targets and the publication of review times as they allow some sort of measurement of performance.

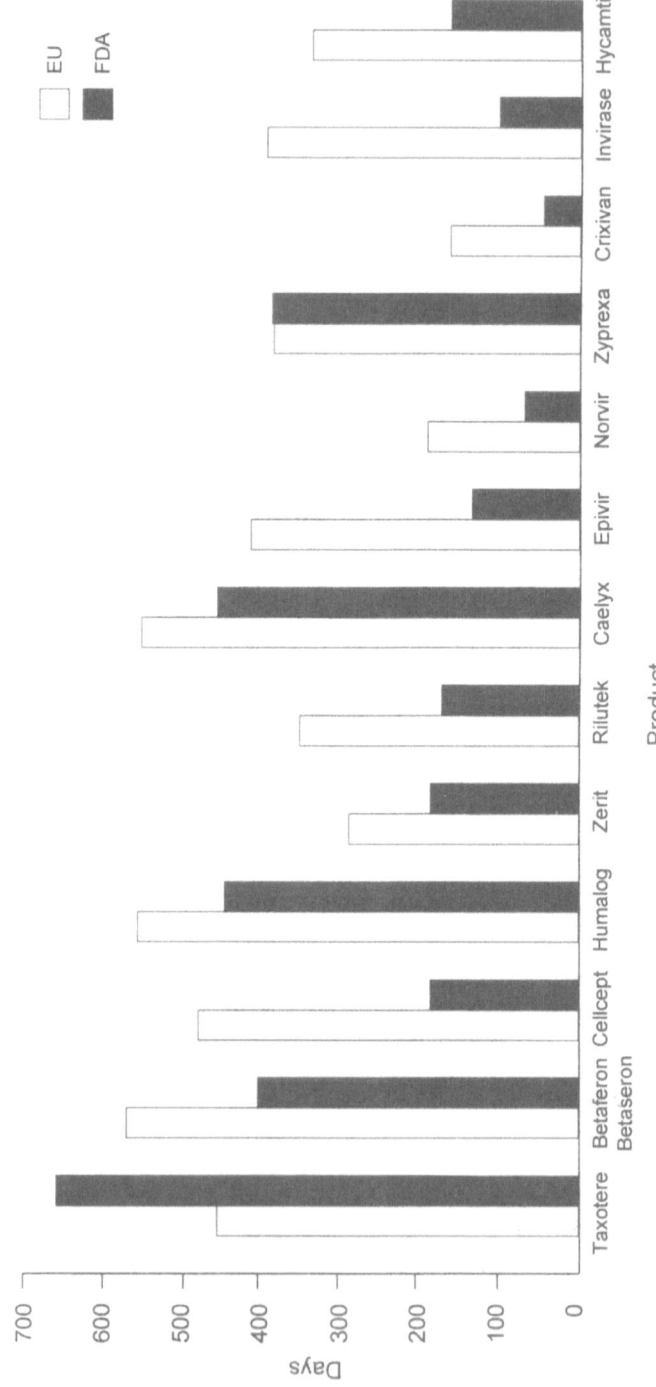

**Figure 8.5** Approval times for products licensed by the EU Centralised Procedure (including concertation) and by the FDA

## Recommendations and conclusions

I believe that targets should be established in Europe for both the processes and the parties involved within those processes, and that includes the industry. It is important to measure performance against targets; the targets are the stretch goals; measurements show whether these goals are being approached. These targets should be transparent and the results of measurements made available. To ensure that there are adequate resources underpinning performance, there is merit in linking fees with performance.

It is important to publish performance data regularly and to identify and celebrate improved performance; this is not done often enough. The FDA has certainly done very well at improving its performance and should be given credit for that. Europe also deserves credit, not only for establishing two new systems but also for remaining operational throughout the evolutionary process. It is also important to check progress against the longer term goals within the strategic objective and to target, on an ongoing basis, further improvement areas and to benchmark agencies around the world. Currently, CMR International is addressing this issue.

In conclusion, targets are necessary in Europe. Target methodology can be inspirational while improving performance and ensuring that continuous improvement becomes built into the regulatory system. With the current complexity in Europe targets are mandatory; they bind the stakeholders together with a common purpose and help to clarify the goals and responsibilities for the different groups that are involved in the regulatory process. They also highlight areas for improvement within the system.

It is important that the agencies around the world are competitive; with transparency of information it will be possible to judge the competitiveness of the different systems. Finally, the definition of targets and performance measurement will enable patients and the medical profession to have access to new and improved medicines as early as is feasible.

# 9 Key milestones in the regulatory review process

KATE THOMAS

## Summary

1.  Leading figures from both industry and regulatory authorities advocated the identification of transparent, defined stages in the review process which could be benchmarked across authorities as a strategy that might be considered for improving the regulatory review process.

2.  The key milestones used in the review processes of nine out of 11 major regulatory authorities have been identified in order to facilitate a more accurate comparison of these processes.

3.  Six key milestones were identified as being applicable to the review processes of all nine authorities providing data for this study, although only one, the date of marketing authorisation application being submitted, is routinely recorded in all cases.

4.  The most important influences on timeliness of the review were considered to be the time taken for the scientific assessment of the dossier, the numbers of internal reviewers employed by the authority, and the use of information technology when processing the application. Quality of the review, on the other hand, was considered to be influenced by reviewer expertise and training, the numbers of meetings between regulatory authority and sponsor, and the outcome of these meetings.

5.  This study detailed the major milestones involved in the review processes of regulatory authorities, and is the first step towards conducting a full-scale benchmarking study of these processes.

6.  Further development will require collaboration between companies and regulatory authorities to monitor the key points in the regulatory approval of compounds submitted simultaneously to multiple authorities. This will aid comparisons of regulatory strategies in order to learn from past successes and to encourage best practice across the international regulatory arena.

## Introduction

There can be considerable variation in the time taken by different regulatory authorities to review submissions for new active substances (NASs), even if the submissions occur in a similar time-frame (McAuslane and Walker, 1996; Thomas *et al.*, 1998). To fully assess the reasons behind these differences, it is essential to determine how the national review processes are monitored and managed. At the eleventh CMR International workshop, held in September 1995, several leading figures from industry and the regulatory authorities advocated the identification of transparent, defined stages in the review process which could be benchmarked across the authorities (Lumley, 1996).

As a consequence of these recommendations, the Centre initiated a study to identify the key milestones used in the review processes of major regulatory authorities, to allow more accurate comparisons of these processes.

Before benchmarking regulatory performance, the milestones currently recorded during the regulatory review process must first be identified and defined and then the key performance indicators and time-lines for the process determined. This paper describes the approach to such a study taken by CMR International, and highlights the milestones commonly used across authorities. By using the study approach described in this paper, a framework will be established that will enable a more accurate comparison of the regulatory processes used by the major regulatory authorities in the review of marketing authorisation applications (MAAs).

These data can then aid the formulation of recommendations on how the review process can best be expedited, by providing a starting point for a more complete understanding of the regulatory review process within different authorities. Such an understanding is essential if the industry and the regulatory authorities are to collaborate in increasing the quality, timeliness, productivity and efficiency of the review process worldwide.

**Table 9.1 Regulatory authorities invited to participate**

| Regulatory authority | Country |
|---|---|
| Therapeutic Goods Administration (TGA) | Australia |
| Health Canada, Therapeutic Products Directorate (TPD) | Canada |
| European Agency for the Evaluation of Medicinal Products (EMEA)* | European Union |
| Agence du Médicament (FMA) | France |
| Federal Institute for Drugs and Medical Devices (BfArM) | Germany |
| Ministry of Health (IMH) | Italy |
| Ministry of Health and Welfare (MHW) | Japan |
| Medicines Evaluation Board (MEB) | Netherlands |
| Medical Products Agency (MPA) | Sweden |
| Medicines Control Agency (MCA) | UK |
| Food and Drug Administration (FDA) Center for Drug Evaluation and Research (CDER) | USA |

*Questioned on the processes employed for the Centralised Procedure

## Methodology

Eleven regulatory authorities (Table 9.1) were invited to participate in this study. Each authority was asked to complete two questionnaires, one describing the procedures involved in producing a national licence for a new active substance and the other, a major variation to an existing marketing authorisation. The questionnaires listed a range of key milestones that were thought likely to apply to each authority's review process (Table 9.2), and respondents were requested to indicate which of the milestones were applicable to their review procedure and, of these, which they currently recorded. In addition, if applicable, the respondents were asked to provide target times for key steps in the process and to indicate, from a given list, what qualitative and quantitative performance indicators they considered to be important in determining the timeliness, productivity or quality of the review (Table 9.3). Finally, information was requested on what resources were available to the authority.

Nine out of the 11 authorities approached provided completed questionnaires on the review process for new active substances. Of these nine, seven also provided completed questionnaires on the review process for variations.

**Table 9.2  Key milestones listed in the questionnaire, and their suggested definitions**

| Description of key milestone | Suggested definitions |
|---|---|
| Marketing authorisation application (MAA) submitted | Date on MAA submitted by the sponsor |
| Valid submission accepted for review | Date on which the MAA was accepted for scientific assessment |
| Start of scientific assessment | Date on which the reviewers started the scientific assessment of the MAA |
| Submission of scientific assessment reports | Date on which the scientific assessment report was signed off by the reviewers |
| Review of the MAA by advisory committee | Date of start of meeting of the advisory committee |
| Regulatory authority requests additional information | Date of letter from regulatory authority requesting clarification or additional information (data or analysis) |
| Response from sponsor | Date of final letter from sponsor providing responses to question(s) as requested by regulatory authority |
| Assessment of response | Date on the final written report, submitted by the reviewer, of the response(s) from the sponsor |
| Regulatory authority grants authorisation | Date when decision is taken that MAA is acceptable |
| Regulatory authority notifies sponsor of decision to grant authorisation | Date of letter issued by the regulatory authority informing sponsor that a product licence will be issued |
| Licensing authority issues product licence | Date on product licence |

**Table 9.3  Suggested influences on timeliness, productivity and quality of the review**

**Quantitative influences on regulatory performance**
Communication:
>Number of meetings with sponsors prior to submission of MAA
>Level of formal contact between reviewers and sponsor during scientific assessments
>Level of informal contact between reviewers and sponsor during scientific assessments

Expertise of reviewers:
>Number of external experts employed in the scientific assessment of MAA
>Number or availability of external experts consulted for scientific advice during the review
>Number of regular in-house seminars and training workshops for existing reviewers
>Size of training budget
>Number of conferences attended by internal reviewers

Resources:
>Total budget for reviews
>Number of internal reviewers
>Number of external reviewers
>Size of support staff

Speed of review:
>The time taken from initial submission of MAA to granting of authorisation
>Time taken for scientific assessment

**Qualitative influences on regulatory performance**
Communication:
>Outcome of meetings with sponsors prior to submission of MAA
>Nature of contact between reviewers and sponsor during scientific assessments
Expertise of reviewers:
>Level of expertise of reviewers
>Formal training programme for new reviewers

Technology:
>Use of information technology (IT) for processing applications, e.g. databases for tracking the application
>Use of information technology (IT) for reviewing applications, e.g. CANDAs

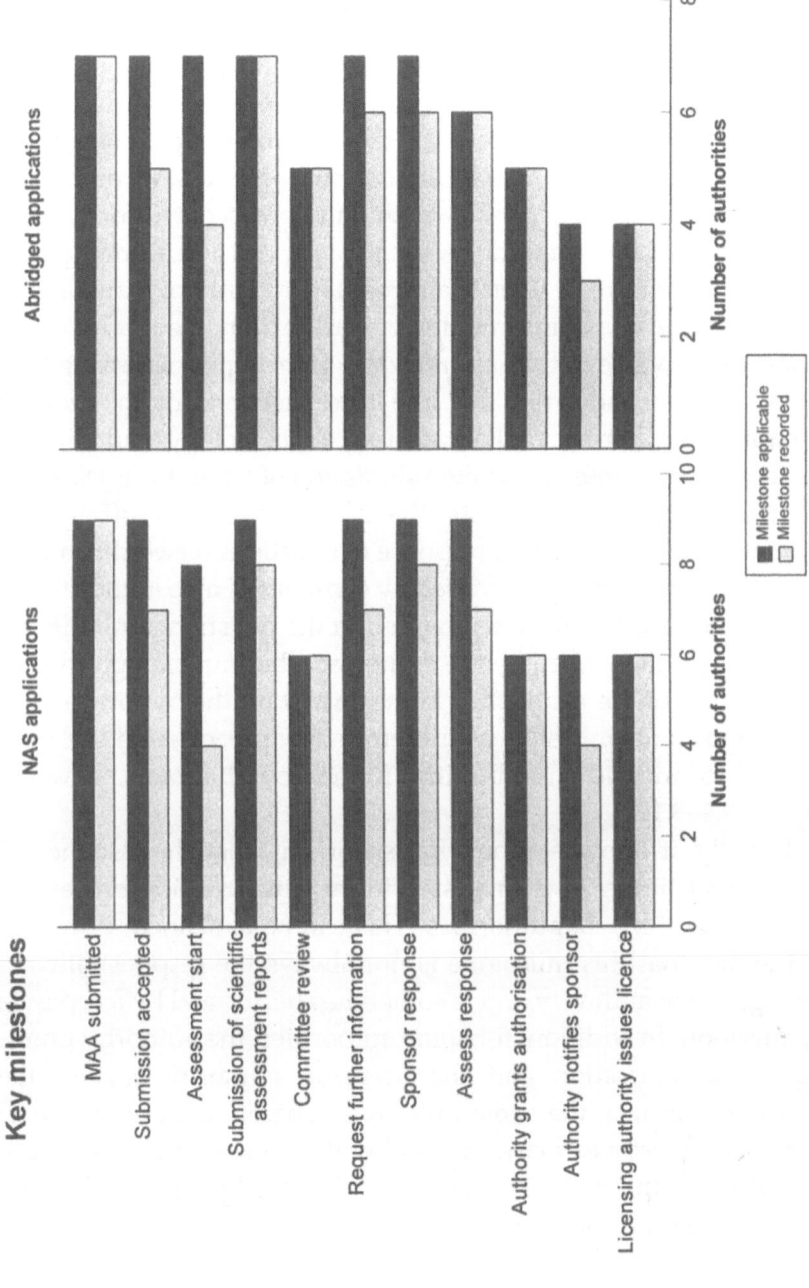

**Figure 9.1** Key milestones in the review process

### New active substances

*Key milestones*

The date of submission of the marketing authorisation application for new active substances is the only key milestone recorded by all authorities (Figure 9.1). However, six milestones were considered by all respondents to be applicable to their review processes, namely: date of submission; date submission accepted for review; date on which the scientific assessment report was signed off by the reviewers; date of letter from regulatory authority to sponsor requesting additional information or clarification; the receipt of the sponsor's response to this; and the date of the report assessing this. All authorities indicated that the three sections of the dossier (chemistry & pharmacy, pharmacology & toxicology, and clinical) are assessed in parallel, and the submission of scientific assessment reports, defined by the date the report is signed off by the reviewer, and the sponsor's response to questions raised during the assessment are currently recorded by eight out of nine authorities.

At times the definitions provided in the questionnaire differed slightly from those used by the authorities, but not enough to alter the meaning of the results. Six authorities took the opportunity to define additional milestones for their review process, and these are detailed for individual authorities in the flow diagrams shown in Figures 9.4–9.12.

Initially, it appears somewhat surprising that the issuance of the product licence, the final step in the authorisation process, is only recorded by six authorities. This can be explained, however, by the fact that this milestone is not always the responsibility of the regulatory authority and is sometimes performed by a separate organisation. In addition, for some authorities, the authority granting the authorisation and the licensing authority issuing the licence are, in fact, the same milestone. Therefore, at least one of these two milestones marks the end of the review process for each regulatory authority participating in this study, and in all cases where these milestones were applicable, they were also recorded.

*Target times*

The target times set by authorities varied enormously (Figures 9.4 – 9.12), both in terms of the parts of the process assigned targets, and the milestones these contained. For example, some authorities set targets for the whole process, and for certain events within the process, others solely set a target for the whole review, whilst yet others set targets just for certain areas of the review. In addition, although most authorities set their time-lines in calendar days, a few use working days to set these targets and, consequently, they are not easily comparable. Although similar areas of the submission have been set time-lines by most authorities, such as time from submission validated to end of initial scientific assessment, the differences in regulatory process between different authorities, for example, where the advisory committee becomes involved in the process, make direct comparisons of the different processes rather complex. Therefore, the milestones and the time-lines set for these milestones are shown on an individual authority basis (Figures 9.4–9.12). Five authorities indicated that they set a target or expected time for the sponsoring company to respond to regulatory questions, and this generally ranged from 60 to 90 calendar days, although one authority said it required an immediate response, and another indicated that the target time was set on a case-by-case basis. In most cases, target times for responding to regulatory questions were flexible, and could be extended upon request.

*Characterising the review procedure*

Of the proposed quantitative characteristics listed in the questionnaire (Table 9.3), a number were considered to influence the timeliness, productivity or quality of the review process. In particular, the size of the review budget was considered to impact all three factors by the majority of authorities.

*Timeliness:* As expected, all authorities linked the amount of time taken by the reviewer to perform the initial scientific assessment with timeliness of the total review procedure for NASs. Other criteria

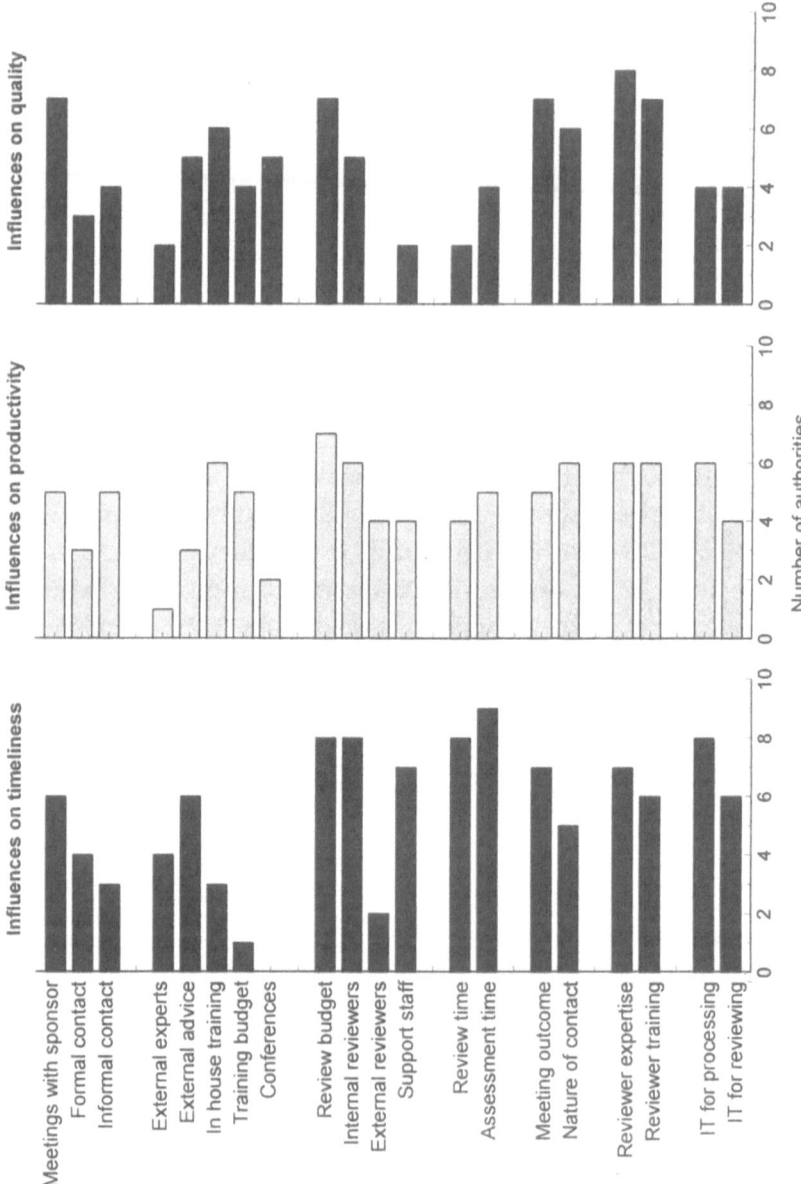

**Figure 9.2** Influences on the timeliness, productivity and quality of the review for NAS applications

**Table 9.4** Additional influences on timeliness, productivity and quality of the review processes for new active substances and variations to existing marketing authorisations (suggested by the participants)

| | *Number of regulatory authorities suggesting this influence* | | |
| --- | --- | --- | --- |
| *Suggested influence* | *Influences timeliness* | *Influences productivity* | *Influences quality* |
| Reviewer workload | 1 | 1 | – |
| Accommodation | 1 | 1 | – |
| Quality, clarity & standardisation of application | 3 | 3 | 2 |
| Quality & clarity of sponsor meetings during development | 1 | 1 | 1 |
| Social climate | 1 | 1 | – |
| Rationale for pricing & reimbursement | 1 | 1 | – |
| Agency structure | 1 | 1 | – |
| Rationale for legal status | 1 | 1 | – |
| Development & compliance with Good Regulatory Practice | 1 | 1 | 1 |

considered to have an important influence on timeliness included the number of internal reviewers, review time and the use of information technology (IT) for processing the application (Figure 9.2).

A number of the study participants suggested additional influences, but particularly the quality, clarity and standardisation of the application were considered important by three authorities. Other influences, which were suggested by just one authority each, are shown in Table 9.4.

*Productivity:* Opinions varied on what determined productivity of the review, with 12 of the 20 listed criteria being marked as important by at least five authorities. The most commonly chosen criterion, however, was the size of the review budget. In addition, six other criteria were deemed important by six authorities and these were the number of regular in-house seminars and workshops for existing reviewers, the numbers of internal reviewers employed, the nature of contact between reviewers and sponsor during the scientific assessment, the level of expertise of reviewers, formal training programmes for reviewers and the use of IT for processing the applications.

*Quality:* In the light of the differences in their approach to contact with the sponsor during the pre-submission phase, an important finding of this study is that most authorities consider that the quality of the review is also influenced by the number of sponsor meetings, and their outcome. In addition, the level of training and of expertise possessed by the reviewer are also considered to impact on review quality.

*Resources*

The data summarised in Table 9.5 highlight differences not only in the resources that are available to the authorities, but also in the authorities' workloads. For example, the number of internal reviewers employed by the authorities ranges from five to 70, with the number of NAS applications submitted in 1996 ranging from 13 to 300.

**Table 9.5  Resources available to regulatory authorities for the review of NAS applications**

| Resource | Number of authorities providing data | Mean | Median | Range |
|---|---|---|---|---|
| Total NAS review budget | 1 | – | – | – |
| Number of internal reviewers | 5 | 37.6 | 38 | 5–70 |
| Number of external reviewers | 4 | 262.5 | 120 | 10–800 |
| Number of advisory committees | 6 | 7.5 | 6.5 | 1–17 |
| Number of support staff | 4 | 26.8 | 20 | 7–60 |
| Number of NAS applications in 1996 | 6 | 84.5 | 50 | 13–300 |

**Variations**

*Key milestones*

In the case of applications for variations to existing marketing authorisations (abridged applications), all seven authorities considered six of the 11 milestones listed in the questionnaire to be applicable to their review processes (Figure 9.1). Only two of these six, the date of MAA submission and submission of the scientific assessment report, are recorded by all authorities. In addition, the dates of requests for additional information, sponsor responses to questions and the assessment of these responses are currently recorded by all but one of the respondents.

*Characterising the review procedure*

In general, opinions on what influences the timeliness, productivity and quality of the review procedure for variations to existing marketing authorisations (Figure 9.3) were proportionally very similar to those relating to the review of NAS applications.

*Timeliness:* The factors most often cited as influencing timeliness of abridged applications were the number of internal reviewers and the reviewers' expertise. Interestingly, the review time was only mentioned by five authorities. Other factors considered to influence the timeliness of the review process by individual authorities were identical to those given in response to the questionnaire for new active substances.

*Productivity:* The number of internal reviewers was also seen as the most important influence on the productivity of the review of variations to existing marketing authorisations, being cited by six authorities. Seven other influences were indicated by five authorities as being important: the in-house training of reviewers, the review budget, assessment time, the nature of contact between reviewer and sponsor, reviewer expertise and reviewer training, and the use of information technology for processing the application.

*Quality:* The main influences on the quality of the review for variations were the levels of reviewer expertise and reviewer training. Other factors that were mentioned were the nature of contact between reviewer and sponsor, outcome of their meetings, size of the review budget, and conferences and in-house training attended by the reviewer.

99

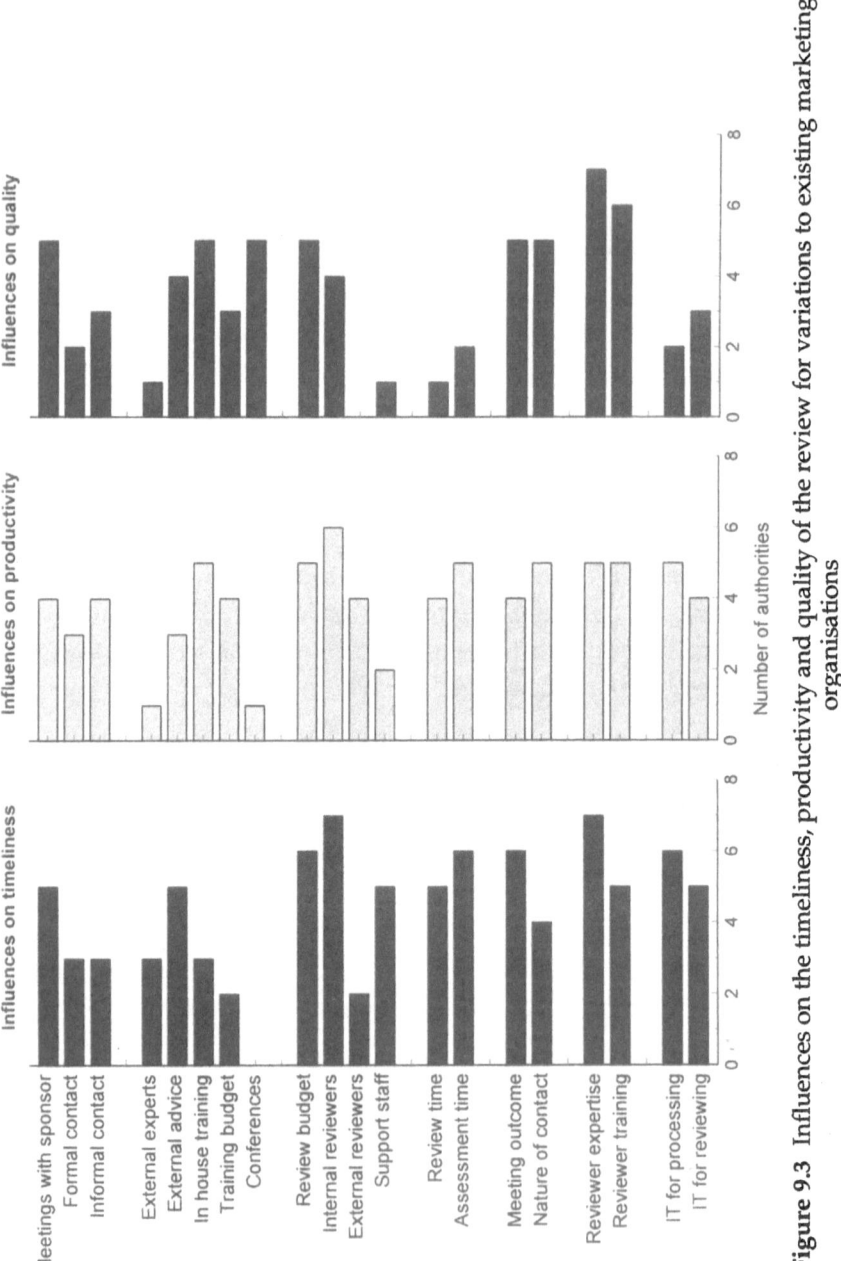

**Figure 9.3** Influences on the timeliness, productivity and quality of the review for variations to existing marketing organisations

*Resources*

The data provided in this section highlight both the wide range in the level of resources available to different regulatory authorities, and the differences in authorities' workloads. In 1996, for the review of variations to existing marketing authorisations, the number of internal reviewers available to work on the submissions ranged from 3 to 70, and the number of applications ranged from 50 to 1790.

## Discussion

This study has attempted to provide an accurate assessment of the milestones involved in the present review processes of regulatory authorities (as shown in Figures 9.4–9.12). Without such information it is impossible to determine where to focus the efforts of any performance improvement initiatives, or how to evaluate progress once these changes are implemented. In addition, such data are required to help regulatory authorities compare elements of their strategies with those of other authorities, in order to learn from past successes and to encourage best practice across the international regulatory arena.

From this study it can be seen that although, at the time of writing, authorities are not collecting and utilising the same data to monitor their own performance, the review processes of all authorities have a number of common milestones. Major procedural changes would not, therefore, be required in order to conduct a study which attempted to benchmark the review processes across authorities using the same decision points or events.

It is also apparent from the present study that the processes themselves are not the only important determinant of a good review. The size of the review budget was mentioned in nearly all cases as being an important determinant of regulatory performance, in terms of productivity, quality and timeliness of the review. This is not surprising, as the financial resources available to an authority will have an impact on all other types of resources available, from numbers of reviewers to information technology resources. Perhaps a more significant finding of this study is the importance placed by the majority of authorities on the meetings between the sponsor and the regulatory authority. In general, these meetings enhance all the qualitative aspects of the review process examined in this study, and this may be one area that can be focused on for improvement in the future. However, to hold meetings between sponsors and the authorities requires a high level of funding and, at the time of writing, many authorities simply do not have the resources to do this. This is illustrated by the study data on the resources available to authorities for conducting reviews. To give a more specific example, the Japanese Ministry of Health and Welfare Pharmaceuticals and Cosmetics Division is staffed by 38 personnel, and charges a user fee of US$ 8,000, whilst in the USA, the user fee for a new drug application is US$ 208,000, and the Center for Drug Evaluation and Research within the FDA employs 741 staff (Misawa, 1996).

Questionnaire-based studies have certain limitations. They are always open to differences in interpretation of the questions by participants, and certain responses may be influenced by the opinions of the person completing the questionnaire, rather than reflecting the position of the regulatory agency as a whole. However, in this study responses were obtained from nine of 11 major international regulatory authorities, and questionnaires were completed by personnel at a very senior level within the authorities.

In the past, accurate comparisons of the review processes of different authorities have proved difficult due to lack of transparency, the large quantities of data involved and the complexity of the processes themselves. The recent investment by authorities in restructuring and re-organising their review processes has focused interest on submission review times and review process management, and many regulatory authorities now publish information on their review performance (MCA Annual Report 1994–95, PDUFA Fourth Annual Performance Report). This increase in the availability of information has led to comparisons being made, where the review times of different regulatory authorities have been broken down and compared (Stroud, 1995). Since regulations and review processes still differ between countries, the usefulness of such studies is limited.

In addition, when looking at current trends in regulatory performance it is important to consider other factors. First, the major responsibility of authorities is towards the protection and promotion of public health and therefore the primary role of regulators must be to assess, as accurately as possible, all potential risks and benefits of any NAS in a marketing authorisation application. Second, the relative availability of resources and information technology are important factors for putting the review times of authorities into context. Finally, it is important to recognise that industry also has a responsibility to maximise the efficiency of the process by presenting good quality dossiers to the regulatory authorities at the outset.

## Conclusions

This study has begun to identify some of the similarities and differences that exist between the review processes of different authorities. This information is essential if further work is to be carried out whereby such processes can be compared in detail.

Future studies will concentrate on collecting data from both companies and regulatory authorities on the review processes. Such co-ordination and working in partnership will facilitate the sharing of information, and will allow authorities to benefit from each other's experience and hence improve performance.

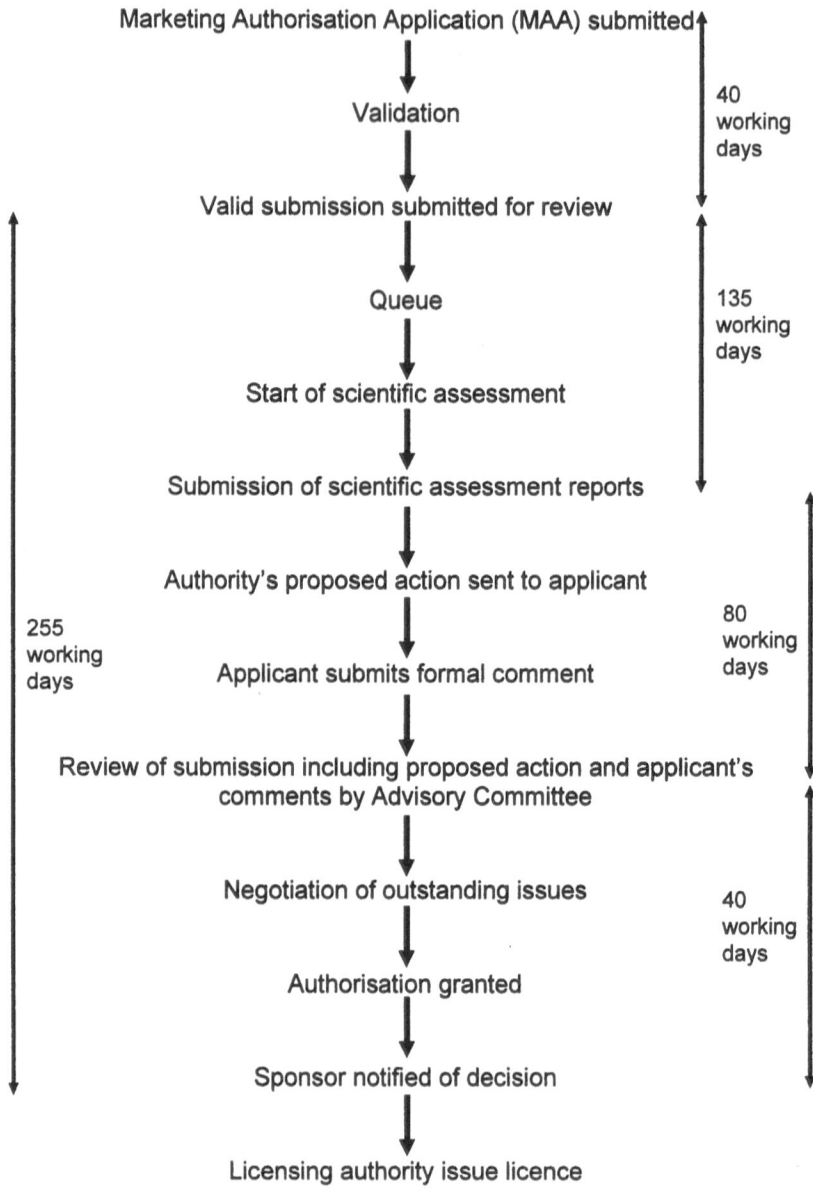

**Figure 9.4** Australian regulatory review process

Key Milestones in the Regulatory Review Process

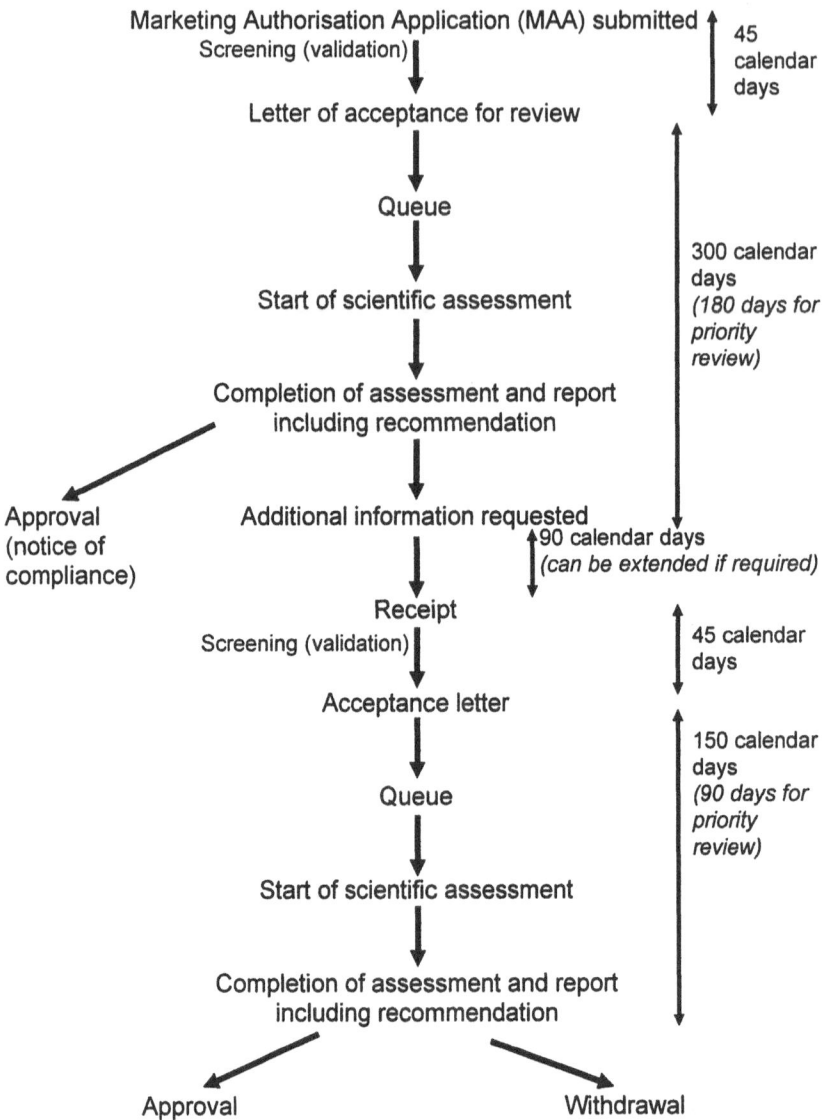

Figure 9.5 Canadian regulatory review process

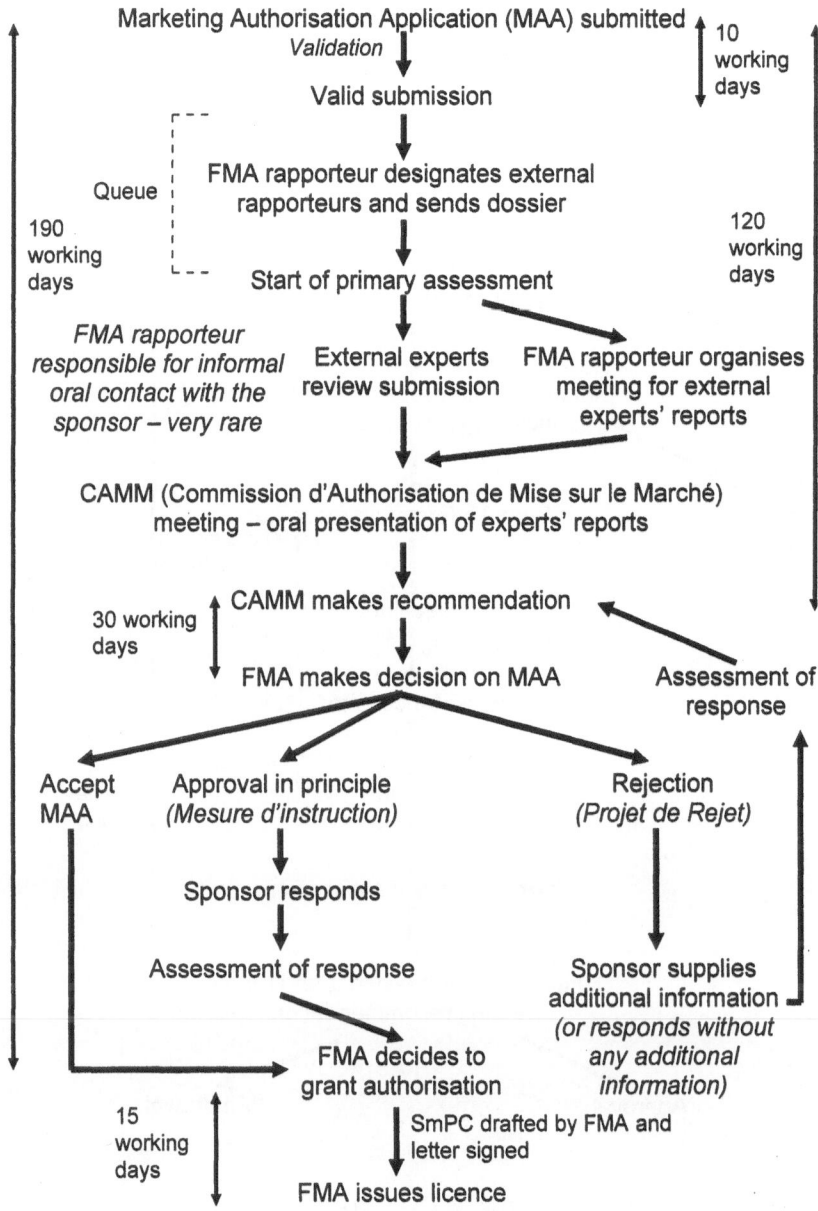

**Figure 9.6** French regulatory review process

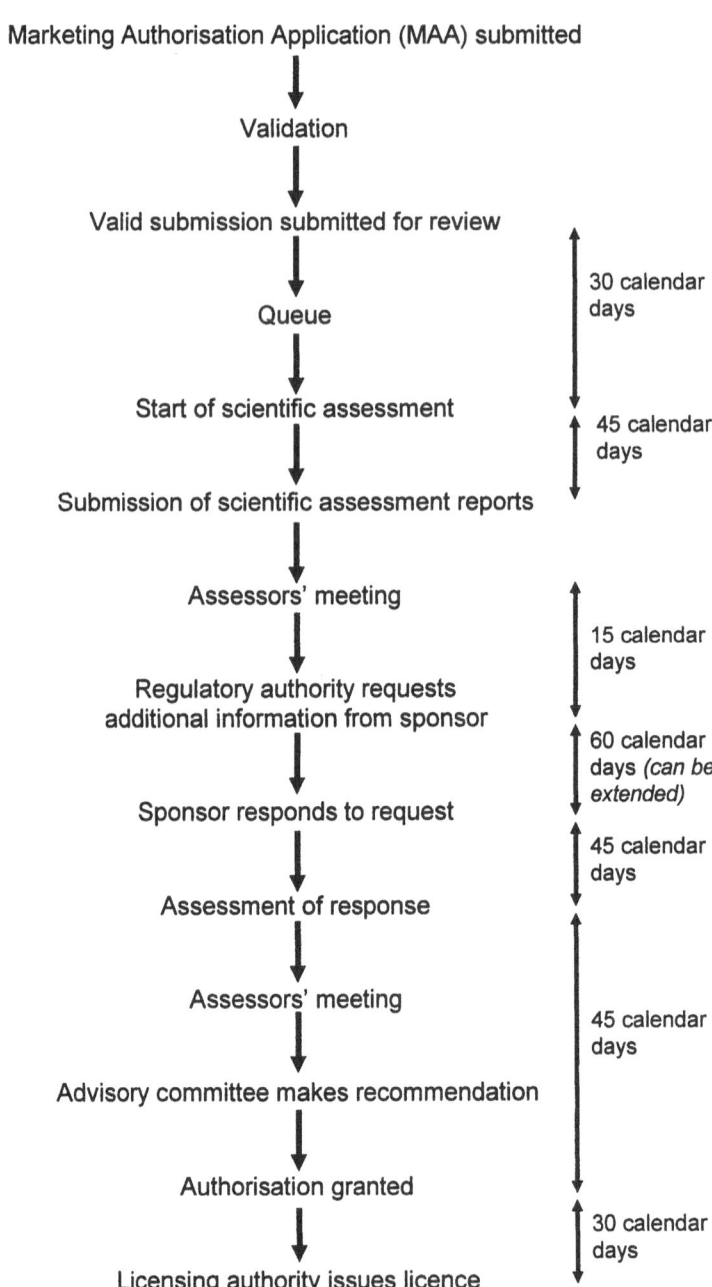

**Figure 9.7** German regulatory review process

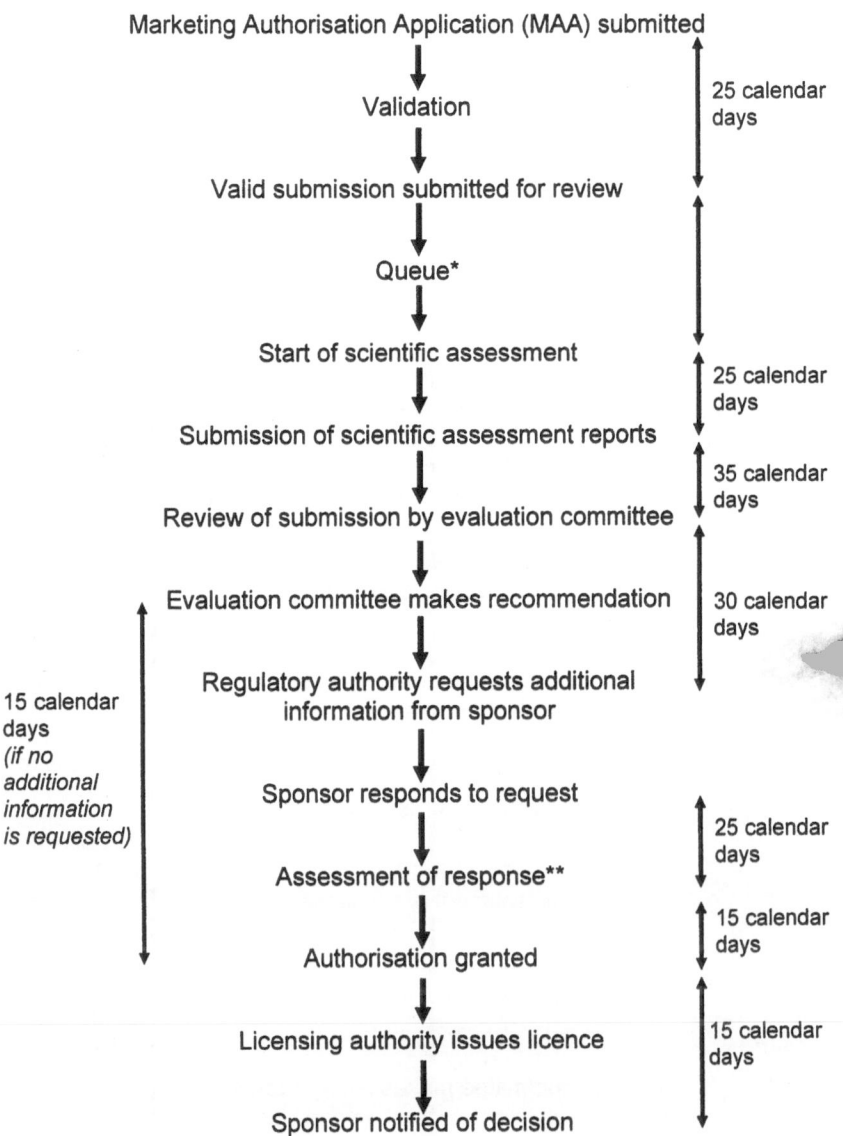

**Figure 9.8**  Italian regulatory review process

*The intended target time for the queue prior to the start of scientific assessment is 30 calendar days. However, due to exceptional circumstances in Italy during the early 1990s, the queuing time is currently longer than this, whilst the authority deals with the backlog of compounds that have built up within the process during this time.

**A slightly longer time may be needed if a new opinion of the evaluation committee is necessary

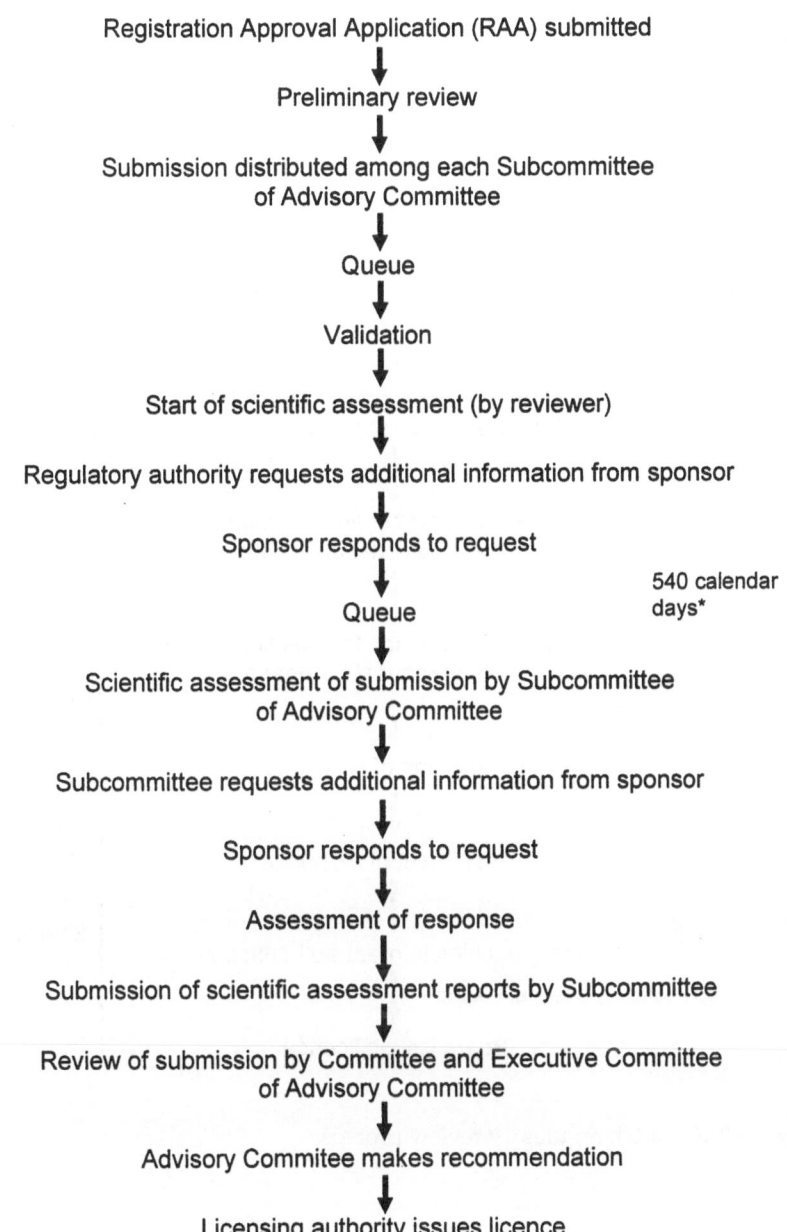

**Figure 9.9** Japanese regulatory review process
*540 calendar days does not include days spent on the side of the applicant

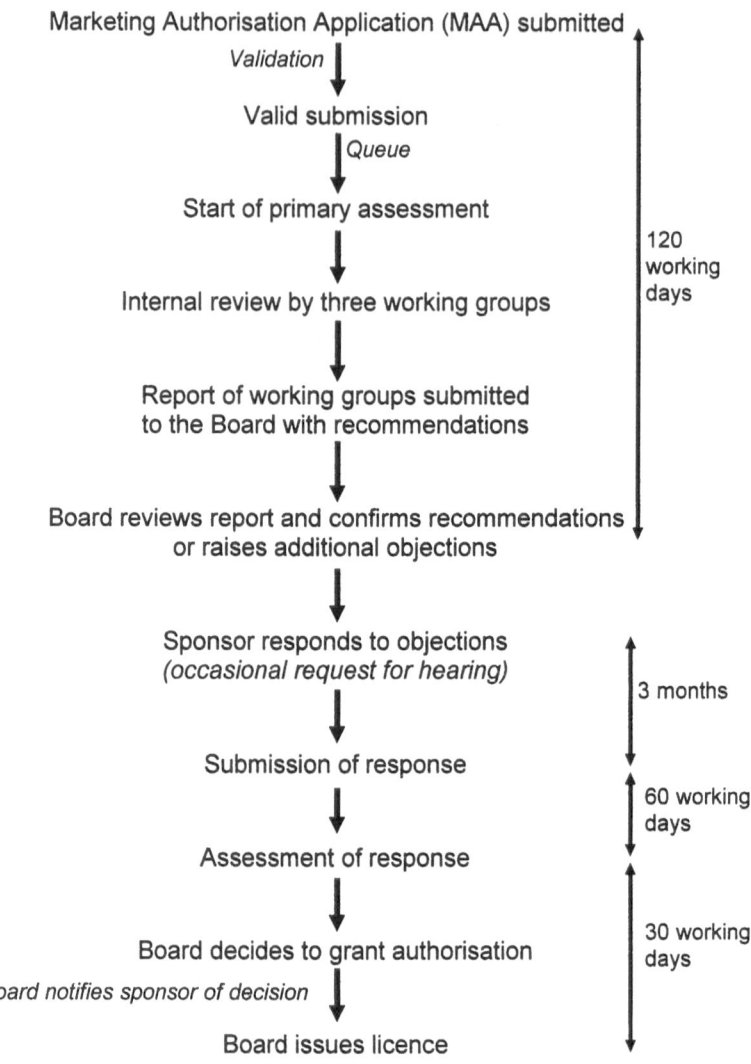

**Figure 9.10** Dutch regulatory review process

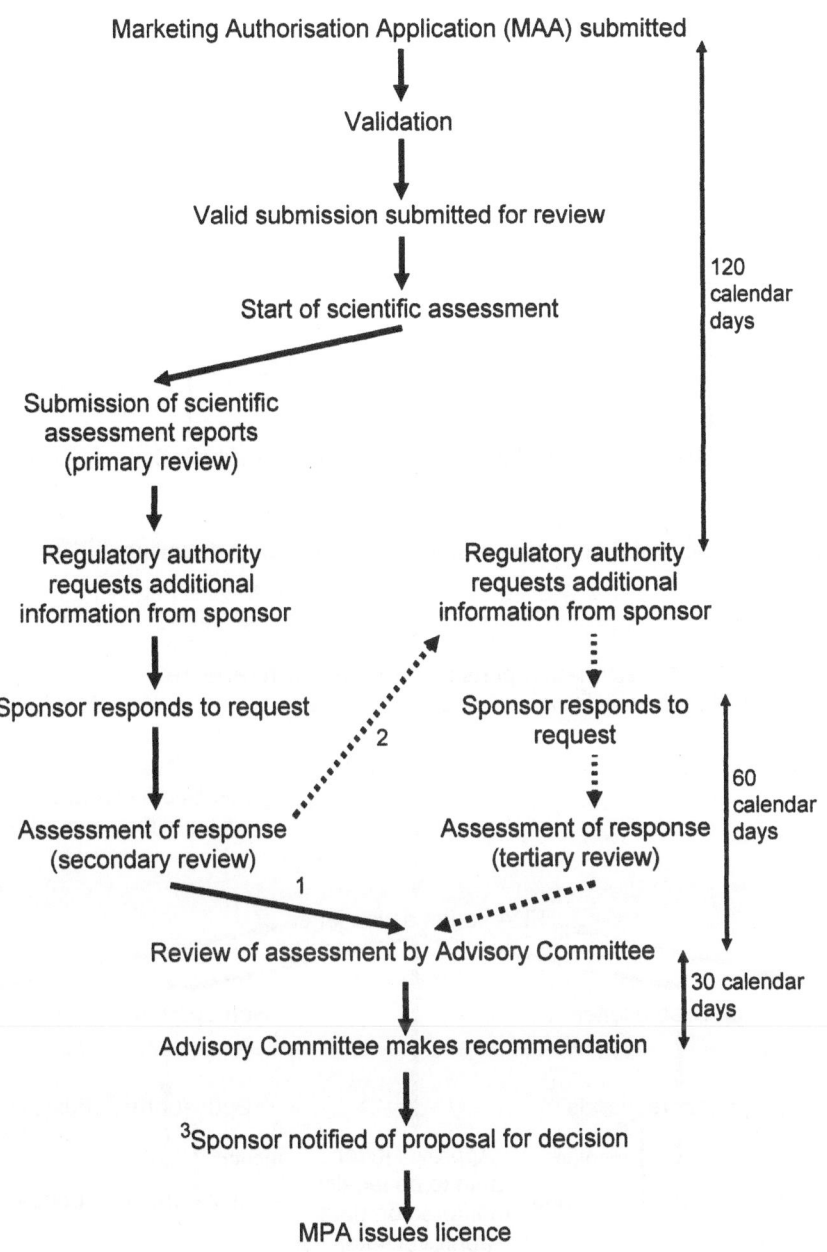

**Figure 9.11** Swedish regulatory review process
[1] Main route; [2] exceptional cases; [3] gives the sponsor the possibility of withdrawal in case of rejection

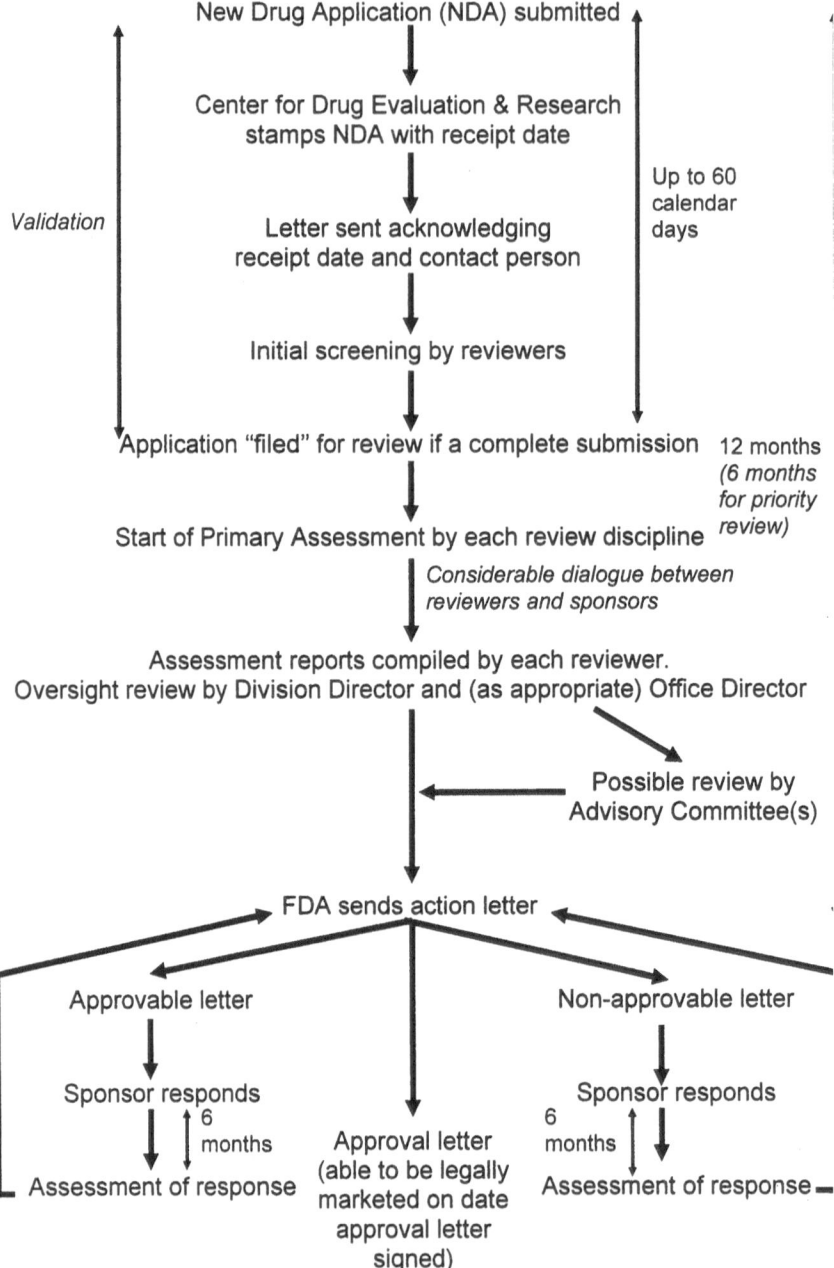

**Figure 9.12** US regulatory review process (CDER)

## References

Lumley CE (1996). Suggestions that might be considered for improving the review process. In: Lumley CE and Walker SR (eds.), *Improving the Regulatory Review Process: Industry and Regulatory Initiatives*, Kluwer Academic Publishers, Dordrecht, pp. 119–130.

McAuslane JAN and Walker SR (1996). International regulatory review times. In: Lumley CE and Walker SR (eds.), *Improving the Regulatory Review Process: Industry and Regulatory Initiatives*, Kluwer Academic Publishers, Dordrecht, pp. 1–12.

Medicines Control Agency Annual Report and Accounts 1995/96, HMSO.

Misawa K (1996). What strategies should be considered for implementation by the end of the century? MHW perspective. In: Lumley CE and Walker SR (eds.), *Improving the Regulatory Review Process: Industry and Regulatory Initiatives*, Kluwer Academic Publishers, Dordrecht, pp. 139–148.

Prescription Drug User Fee Act of 1992. Fiscal Year 1996 Report to Congress. December 1996. Food and Drug Administration, Department of Health and Human Services.

Stroud R Consulting Inc (1995). Drug Submission Evaluation: International comparison of performance standards and performance. Report and study commissioned by Health Canada.

Thomas KE, McAuslane JAN, Parkinson C, Luscombe DK and Walker SR (1998). A study of trends in pharmaceutical regulatory approval times for 9 major markets in the 1990's. *Drug Information Journal*, **32** (2), May 1998.

# 10 How do you measure the quality of the scientific assessment and the review process? The view of the MCA

DAVID JEFFERYS

**Summary**

1.  Drug regulators are increasingly focusing on the effectiveness of the regulatory process, to ensure the protection of the public health. The quality of decision making and thereby the effectiveness of drug regulation is far more difficult to measure and audit than the efficiency of the process.

2.  The key elements of the review process are the summarisation of data, the critical analysis of information and the decision process. The quality of the activity has to be built in at each stage of the process.

3.  In Europe the Assessment Report Guideline serves as a standard operating procedure. As self-standing documents supported by audit trails, assessment reports permit secondary assessment by concerned Member States in the Mutual Recognition Procedure and by non-rapporteur Member States in the Centralised Procedure.

4.  The building of a single community system in Europe provides a unique opportunity for quality assurance between regulators, a major public health benefit.

5.  The challenge to regulators and industry is to examine, together, the new review process being created and ensure that the right standards are set to achieve effective drug regulation.

## Changing emphasis

During the first half of this decade the focus of attention has been on improving the efficiency of the drug regulatory process. Over this period there has been a significant improvement in the assessment times which can be attributed to improved use of resources, new management systems, new IT support and greater dialogue between the regulator and the regulated. More recently, attention has focused on the benefits of fast-track assessments, accelerated reviews and increased dialogue during the development phase.

Increasingly, drug regulators have been concerned to improve the effectiveness of the process, although this has received less discussion so far. Ensuring the quality of decision making and thereby the effectiveness of drug regulation is important to all stakeholders, in particular, patients, the professions and the pharmaceutical industry.

Efficiency and effectiveness of the regulatory process are linked. Behind increased efficiency – better value for money, and better time-lines – lies effectiveness, a far more difficult issue to address. There are two ways it could be considered; speed of the overall review time or quality of the output in terms of the SmPC (summary of product characteristics). For instance, what may be perceived by the industry as relatively minor changes in labelling can make the difference between a successful, safe product or one that is unsafely used by patients, perhaps leading to restrictions or withdrawal.

## Identifying underlying issues

'Are we regulating effectively and safely?' is the underlying question. The prime function of regulators is to protect and safeguard the public health. Speed to market is clearly an important component, since if the regulatory process is slow the public and the professions are being denied effective medicines. However, if less effective medicines are allowed onto the market then this too has an impact on healthcare delivery.

The industry and the regulators should examine the review process that has been created. Is the control point right? Does the process need re-engineering now that many of the agencies around the world are probably achieving the optimum speed of review? Can the speed of the overall process be improved by focusing on other elements, earlier in development? In addition, are there different expectations between the regulators and the regulated which may account for the relatively high attrition rate during the approval process? These fundamental issues may generate a greater return than overdue concentration on further speeding up the review process.

## Key elements of the review process

The drug review process involves three separate, but interlinked, elements (Table 10.1), of which the first is a summary of the data. From a European perspective, regulators would like to see industry doing more of the summarisation, as required by the Draft Notice to Applicants (November 1994). This in itself would increase the efficiency of the process.

**Table 10.1  Components of the drug review process**

| |
|---|
| • Summary of the presented data |
| • Critical analysis of: |

| | |
|---|---|
| Information | – presented in the dossier |
| | – derived from the dossier |
| | – SmPC |
| Decision | – authorisation |

The prime job of reviewers is the critical analysis of *information*, not data, as presented in the dossier and, on occasions, derived by further statistical analysis. European regulators are assisted in this task by the EC Assessment Report Guideline issued in late 1994.

This acts as a standard operating procedure, to be used in both the Centralised and the Mutual Recognition Procedures.

*EC Assessment Report Guideline*

A key feature of the guideline is the creation of a free-standing document, essential for an effective process in Europe. This allows a targeted (or secondary) assessment by concerned Member States around the assessment report of the Reference Member State in the Mutual Recognition Procedure. In the Centralised Procedure it allows the CPMP members and therefore the national authorities to take a targeted view of the assessment report of the rapporteur and co-rapporteur. It was never the intention, nor is it the practice of most Member States, to re-analyse the data.

The guideline stresses the need for peer review and for quality assurance programmes to be built into the regulatory process. It also stipulates that an audit trail be provided so that the assessment report is auditable both by the other Member States and by the applicant. The option for the applicant to provide feedback, if there is misrepresentation of the data, is an important element of quality control.

The applicant has a critical role. In addition to the expert report process, the innovator must supply a narrative summary, including a global safety analysis for all new drugs and all abridged applications. The role and emphasis of the assessor should therefore change, since the assessor will be judging the accuracy of the summary from the applicant. At present, however, the summaries are often inadequate for this purpose and do not facilitate their incorporation into a free-standing assessment report. There is still much redundancy in this area and greater quality control of the regulatory process within companies is needed. There is little doubt that bad dossiers make for longer and more difficult assessments.

**Table 10.2  MCA response**

---

- Combined approach
  - Build quality into the process
  - Internal reviews – sign offs
  - External peer reviews (advisory committees)
  - Selective audits
  - Quality assurance panels
  - Education and analysis meetings
  - *Post hoc* safety reviews

---

## Approach to quality

Quality is not one item, but needs to be addressed in a multifactorial way. The major factor is to build quality, from within, into each stage of the process and this approach has to be taken for the whole organisation. In the MCA (Medicines Control Agency) various techniques are used (Table 10.2). Sign offs ensure that assessment reports are checked at multiple levels. The majority of external peer reviews occur through external advisory committees but there are other options too.

The approach within Europe and, indeed, worldwide to incorporating quality into the review process starts with a need for guidelines (Table 10.3) and that is why the Assessment Report Guideline for Europe is so critical. All agencies have standard operating procedures for elements of the review process and

**Table 10.3  Incorporation of quality into the review process**

---

- Assessment Report Guideline

- Standard operating procedures

- Horizontal and vertical guidelines

- Training

- IT/IS support

- Quality accreditation

---

119

increasingly these are likely to be shared and incorporated within the European process.

The vertical and horizontal guidelines in Europe allow the agencies to check their review and indicate if, and where, there is any deviation from the guidelines. In this way there is feedback to other bodies, and an indication that a guideline may be out-dated and may need changing.

The increasing need for training, and the need to share this across Europe, is well recognised. Quality also depends very much on IT/IS support, not least for ensuring consistency of approach. It is very important for a regulated industry that consistency is applied and consistent health decisions emerge.

### Assessment of the critical analysis

How can quality be brought into the critical analysis and how can it be measured? Internal review will always be fundamental and this can be approached with either selected audits or full audits. Neither is cheap; at times there will be a need for parallel assessments. In the MCA this occurs for audits in the clinical trials area where an audit team will compare and contrast the decisions of the original reviews. Internal review also involves the sign off, with senior members of staff checking decisions and the reports.

Independent advisory committees have a significant role to play in external peer review. However, with time, these committees can come to reflect the agencies and assessors they work with, or *vice versa*, and this factor should be recognised.

### Decision-making process

The decision stage is a more difficult one to audit because there are inevitably subjective elements. To ensure that decisions reflect the report, and that they are valid and consistent, the MCA uses a variety of approaches (Table 10.4), including selected audits and regular *post hoc* educational and analysis discussions.

*Post hoc* safety reviews are used to consider and re-assess any drug which has been withdrawn from the market for safety

120

**Table 10.4  Assessment of the decision process**

- Selected audits

- *Post hoc* educational and analysis discussions

- Comparative reviews

- *Post hoc* safety reviews

- Consistency reviews

reasons. The objective for such a review is to ascertain the lessons which can be learnt and any failings in the initial regulatory review. A consistent regulatory approach is particularly important in the area of patient information leaflets, so consistency reviews are conducted both retrospectively and prospectively, where a large sample of leaflets is checked across the Agency.

Outcome analysis is an important tool for monitoring the quality of performance. In addition to analysis of safety withdrawals it is also helpful to consider the drug withdrawal rates over a period of time and any major changes in the indications or dose. In such reviews not only is the assessment process being evaluated, but so too is the drug development pursued by the innovator.

There is still much work to be done in this area of overall analysis. It is superficial to rely on benchmarking and time to market. If the quality of performance is to be examined completely then much more attention must be paid, by regulators and industry alike, to reviewing past changes and decisions. It is easy to announce a decision quickly, but is it the right decision? This is a challenge for everyone.

**Europe**

The potential for quality assurance between regulatory authorities in Europe was recognised in 1991 by the Pharmaceutical Evaluation Report (PER) Committee which introduced a questionnaire between the participating countries when an assessment report was exchanged. It was hoped that this would yield valuable feedback on the regulatory procedure. In the event, the response was rather disappointing and little valuable information has been gained. This approach was also extended to the Concertation Procedure, but with similar results.

However, the building of a single community procedure in Europe now offers a unique opportunity for quality assurance. Not only does the guideline reinforce this objective but also the Centralised and Mutual Recognition Procedures together provide an excellent system for quality assurance, with all parties being well informed and vigilant. The net result is high quality SmPCs and high quality reviews. This is one of the major public health benefits of the single community system in Europe.

The new European procedures provide a unique opportunity for quality assurance, both for the protection of the public health and also to act as a quality review and benchmarking exercise between the Member States. A full audit of the regulatory process within a Member State is resource intensive. However, in both the Community systems one has an opportunity for a very sensitive quality assurance review to take place between the participants. In the Mutual Recognition Procedure the concerned Member States have received the full dossier and will be undertaking their own reviews of that assessment. They are in possession of the dossier so that, in a very real sense, they are auditing the assessment of the first or Reference Member State. Similarly, in the Centralised Procedure a full assessment is undertaken by the rapporteur and the co-rapporteur independently and then the other Member State delegations are commenting on the two assessment reports, again having access to the full dossier if necessary and their own review teams.

The challenge for regulators in Europe over the rest of the decade is to work together not only to complete the programme on harmonisation, but also to set the right standards for public health. The possibility of comparing and contrasting approaches across the Member States is both the opportunity and the challenge. It will be important to prevent escalating the regulatory requirements to a level that is inappropriate for the medicines being put forward, which would be to the detriment of the industry and, more importantly, the public health.

## Conclusion

Measuring and assuring the quality of the regulatory review process is indeed a difficult issue for which there is no single answer at present. A partnership approach is needed to reassess the process, and the new system in Europe should be used to respond to these challenges.

# 11 Ensuring the quality of the scientific assessment and the review process: The FDA's good review practice initiative

MURRAY LUMPKIN

**Summary**

1. The FDA is in the process of developing good review practice (GRP) guidance for use within CDER and CBER in order to facilitate the review process and ensure consistency in approach and quality across divisions.

2. In particular, the goal of GRP track VIII is to produce a guidance document for the clinical/statistical reviewer, detailing all the steps in the review process. These fall within three elements, the internal (or reactive) review, the external (or creative) review, and the documentation and conclusion.

3. Each individual study review is composed of three separable but related tasks, the description, auditing and checking, and analysis and evaluation. The track VIII GRP will provide guidance on how to draw such information into an integrated analysis and conclusion regarding safety and efficacy.

4. Once finalised, the GRP documents will be a considerable aid to reviewers and will enhance the quality of the review process.

## Introduction

Over the years, regulatory agencies have been relatively remiss about considering how to build quality into the review process. As industry has good practices for manufacturing (GMP), laboratory work (GLP) and clinical research (GCP), the FDA is devising good review practices (GRP). This thinking is timely, as Food and Drug Administration (FDA) activities are being closely examined and the emphasis on timeliness creates an even greater need for quality assurance through description and documentation of the process. In addition, expansion of reviewing divisions calls for consistency in quality and process across yet more review components. Finally, it is difficult to talk about harmonisation between agencies without knowing exactly what is being done in the process we call 'application review'.

## Evolution of good review practices

Early discussion revealed that the job of the reviewer is not clearly documented. Currently available guidance, such as the FDA's clinical and statistics primary review guideline or the ICH clinical study report guideline, is oriented towards industry's input not the reviewer's output. A large working group within the Center for Biologics Evaluation and Research (CBER) and the Center for Drug Evaluation and Research (CDER), therefore proposed a host of ideas, including the need to adopt good review practices. The four GRP tracks on which initial effort has been concentrated are shown in Table 11.1.

Track XI deals primarily with reviewer training and with mentoring activities; it is essentially complete.

## Development of track VIII

The goals for track VIII are to produce a guideline for the clinical/statistical reviewer that will tell him/her what to do at the outset and how to decide when they have done enough. It is easy to ask questions indefinitely; people need a framework so that

**Table 11.1  Good review practice (GRP) tracks**

| | |
|---|---|
| II | Mechanisms for updating and improving the review process |
| IV | Guideline for the clinical review of an investigational application |
| VIII | Guideline for the clinical review of a marketing application |
| XI | Reviewer interaction, training and communication |

they know when they have fulfilled their duty as a reviewer. Although the guidance document will be oriented to reviewers, it will be a public document and, hopefully, will help sponsors prepare better applications.

In order to produce this guidance document, six working groups have the task to produce an annotated outline of an entire review, identifying all the elements (described in the following sections), the sort of auditing/checking that should be undertaken and the analyses to consider. This task has been divided into six parts: description of the individual study; auditing; analysis of individual studies; integrated summary of effectiveness; documentation; integrated summary of safety. The last of these is now in the public domain and the summary of effectiveness document should follow shortly.

*Reasons for a review*

In developing track VIII guidance, it has been helpful to ask some fundamental questions, such as what is the reason for a review, what are the benefits to the public, what is the value added by the process? Certainly, to ascertain what the data actually show and so protect against over-optimism, deception, incompleteness or lack of inquisitiveness is one answer. Another is to provide assurance that a drug does what is claimed and that the claim is meaningful while sparing avoidable side-effects, and avoiding useless treatments that might otherwise threaten valuable ones. There is also the need for assurance that reasonable effort is being made to find adverse consequences of treatment and to ensure dosing is rational.

**Table 11.2  Functions of a primary review**

- Legal – does application meet test of law?

- Public record – basis for public confidence needs not only to be right but coherent, well organised, and credible

- Public health/scientific element – most detailed review, secondary reviewers depend on it, only review of actual data, details of conduct of studies; review what *is* there and what is not; if inaccurate, incompetent, incomplete, could lead to wrong decision

- Comprehensive evaluation – needs to be complete; standard elements described to avoid need for every review to re-invent, implying need to specify format *and* content (to a degree)

*Functions of a primary review*

The primary review serves a number of functions (Table 11.2); as a public record it needs not only to be right but also coherent, well organised and credible. As the most detailed, and only, review of the actual raw data, secondary reviewers depend upon it; clearly if the primary review is inaccurate, incompetent or incomplete it may lead to a wrong decision. At the same time it must provide a comprehensive evaluation with the standard elements described.

*Elements of a review*

There are three components of a review that must be considered in good review practice guidance. The first is the internal, or reactive, review which means dealing with what has been provided on its own terms, measuring it against the legal standards and guidance but letting the sponsor frame the areas for discussion and examination. To answer the well known questions (Table 11.3) requires intelligence and experience but not necessarily a lot of specialised knowledge. That comes into the second component of the review.

This second, external or creative, review asks questions about what should have been done and submitted, and includes questions the reviewer thinks should really be asked and have not been

**Table 11.3  Internal (reactive) review**

---

Dealing with what has been provided in its own terms, measuring against legal standard and guidance, but letting the sponsor frame the areas for discussion and examination:

- Are the submitted studies adequate and well controlled?

- Were they conducted properly?

- Can analyses be verified?

- Do the studies show the effect claimed, i.e. are the analyses reasonable?

- Does labelling reflect the data?

---

asked by the sponsor. In doing so the reviewer must supply consideration of a number of underlying issues, as shown in Table 11.4.

Good review practices are about the process *and* the document. Therefore, the third element of the review is the documentation and conclusion. This must show what was done and how it fulfilled various requirements (Table 11.5). The implication is that the review must not only be comprehensive but also must distinguish between sponsor's words and reviewer's words, be logical and provide a good index, describe critical review decisions and, if needed, include a problem list.

*Specific tasks within the review*

Most data are described within individual reports of studies or integrated summaries of effectiveness and safety, supported by tabular listings and case record forms. A review can be seen as a specific series of tasks that apply to those reports, summaries and raw data records, while keeping in mind the internal/external distinction.

There are three separable but related tasks: (a) description, (b) verifying, auditing and checking, (c) critical analysis and evaluation.

**Table 11.4  External (creative) review: Considerations**

Need also to ask about what could or should have been done and submitted, questions not usually addressed in the application and not answerable by further analyses. The reviewer must supply these considerations:

- Are study endpoints appropriate, clinically meaningful, an accepted surrogate?

- Is the study design suitable (not just well controlled): long enough, right control group, right population?

- Is there adequate exposure of population subsets?

- Is the safety data base adequate (all tests reasonably applicable: total exposure, duration, particular laboratory or other tests, broad enough population, proper dose finding)?

- Was there human exploration/follow-up of toxicological findings?

- Was there an assessment of possible drug–drug or drug–disease interactions?

- Are there expected uses that sponsor should be studying? (Adequate directions for use.)

The descriptive component is critical so that the secondary reviewer can conduct their tasks; omissions are extremely problematic. The description presents what the sponsor has done and concluded in addition to what has been found by the reviewer, noting ambiguities, in considerable detail for important studies. A list of points to be covered in the description has been proposed for inclusion in the track VIII GRP guidance. This will allow a reviewer to see whether a study *could* be adequate and well controlled, and show evidence of effectiveness, and whether it *could* meet regulatory guidances. But did it? That question must be addressed next, through the external review, by identifying potential omissions or unclear sections in the description.

The type of activities performed under the second task, verifying, auditing and checking, to confirm the accuracy of the spon-

**Table 11.5  Documentation and conclusions**

---

The review must document, for next level or future reviewers:

- The critical data reviewed

- What reviewer did to verify and analyse

- Results of reviewer's review and analysis

- Any information not pursued and reason

- Conclusions, including questions and problems (further analyses, data needed)

Review must show fulfilment of all relevant legal, medical, policy requirements.

---

**Table 11.6  Specific tasks within the review**

---

*Verifying, auditing, checking:*

Several elements:

- On-site inspection

- Compliance with protocol
  - minutes of Data and Safety Monitoring Boards (DSMBs)
  - appearance of test and control drugs
  - reason for drop-outs

- Transfer of data from case record forms to tabulations

- Deciding whether endpoint occurred according to pre-set standard

- Verification of analyses; can tabular data be used to replicate results?

---

131

**Table 11.7 Conclusions**

Risk/benefit judgement

- Substantial evidence of effectiveness (one study special case)

- Clinical relevance of clinical or surrogate endpoint

- Adequacy of effect size

- Adequacy of safety assessment

- Acceptability of ADRs in relation to benefit

- Need for limitation of use, by labelling, to subset

- Special monitoring (accelerated approval)

- Adequate directions for use

- Further studies post-marketing

---

sor's description at many levels, are shown in Table 11.6. Then follows the analysis and evaluation part, where key questions must be addressed: is the study adequate and well controlled, is the description clear, was the design adequate, appropriate and verifiable, was bias in conduct and analysis minimised adequately, and are the conclusions scientifically sound?

Such an approach focuses on the individual study; however, in the end, much of what a reviewer must do relates to integrated analysis and conclusions about safety and effectiveness. Therefore, the track VIII guidance will also address how to bring about this integration of the major data sources and outcomes and looking at both the analysis of what was submitted and what was not. This leads to the overall conclusions, based on a risk/benefit judgement (Table 11.7).

When it comes to documenting a review, decisions have to be made on how much sponsor-generated material to include and how to document the choices made, material considered or ignored, and case record forms reviewed. For track VIII guidance, there is a desire to approach this from a problem-oriented perspective, with a standard structure and numbering system and a standard approach to labelling.

## Comment

This review summarises the thinking behind the good review practices initiative and describes what we want to achieve. Once finalised, we hope these documents will be a great help to the reviewer and further enhance the quality of the review process.

# 12 Outcome of syndicate discussions

NEIL McAUSLANE and STUART WALKER

## Introduction

The presentations and discussions throughout the workshop focused on current regulatory reforms and improvements in the review process, the importance of setting targets and how the issue of quality should be addressed. These set the scene for the main objective of the workshop which was to bring regulators and industry together to define "mutually agreeable performance measures and targets for the review process" and to determine "the appropriate measures of the quality of the review". The participants were divided into four syndicate groups, two to consider performance measures and two to consider quality. The groups were to asked discuss the issues and, subsequently, to present to all participants, via a rapporteur, the outcome of their deliberations.

These discussions and the outcome of the final feedback session indicated that more could be done to define performance measures, compare data across agencies and build quality into the review. However, the underlying theme was one of concern to ensure that any improvements in speed would not sacrifice quality and that, perhaps, more is required than just streamlining existing processes. In the time available it was not possible to produce a mutually agreed list of specific recommendations. However, a number of suggestions were put forward and there was general agreement by both industry and regulatory representatives on what is required to ensure that improvements are made in assessing the performance and quality of the review. The following sections present the main points made by the rapporteurs on these two issues.

135

## Define mutually agreeable performance measures and targets for the review process for authorising NMEs and abridged applications

### Introduction

The two syndicate groups addressing this topic had wide-ranging discussions which contained many similarities. The questions that were discussed included: why is there a need for mutually agreeable performance measures, what might be measured, and who should be responsible for undertaking such measurements? There was agreement that both the regulators and the regulated have a common interest, albeit with different responsibilities. However, the functions and features of performance measures have to be identified before they can be measured. Each should reflect what is needed to monitor the review process effectively. In particular, performance, speed, efficiency and productivity are paramount in relation to the authorisation of marketing applications.

### Activities that can be measured

The syndicate groups had been provided with the results of the CMR International survey which had identified those milestones that apply to, and are recorded by, the major regulatory authorities (see Chapter 9). Views expressed by the participants indicated that the milestones highlighted in the survey were the key ones but there was some debate on what other milestones might be measured. These included activities prior to filing, as well as presubmission meetings. While emphasising that it may be difficult to compare practices across authorities, as such activities are differently resourced, it was suggested that the use of pre-submission meetings may influence the review procedure. Suggestions of other activities that could be benchmarked included time to first human dose or IND (investigational new drug), and time to scientific advice following a request. Although similar, these are monitored differently by authorities and therefore cannot be compared directly. Some activities may only be a part of the review process, such as translation of documents, hearings/appeals, and post-scientific review. As not all of these are uniform practices it would be difficult to set targets and performance goals for such activities across authorities. However, it could be valuable to monitor them internally within an authority in order to improve our understanding of the processes involved.

Validation of the dossier was highlighted as one activity for which a better understanding is required. This should include what is understood by validation, how long it takes, how it is performed and what are the possible outcomes. This topic was identified as an important issue, and milestones at the start and completion of validation are key to assessing performance in this area.

Although there are a number of milestones and activities that could be benchmarked, the need to have comparability across authorities was stressed. It was proposed that until there is a better understanding of the background to different regulatory processes, the milestones must be unambiguous. Clearly falling into this category are the submission date of an application, indicated by the date of receipt by the authority, and the date a company can legally market the medicine. These mark the beginning and end of the process. Although needing clarification, there is probably an important step in the middle, namely the end of the scientific review.

Concerns were expressed that using the milestone of legal marketing approval ignores the problem in some European countries where the issues of pricing and reimbursement for medications can delay marketing. However, it was believed that product launch should not be benchmarked across regions as there are influences and hurdles to be overcome that are beyond the regulatory authorities' control.

### Measures of performance

The purpose of benchmarking is to monitor the process and identify how long it takes. By setting targets, the intention is to improve the time taken, and/or productivity. Once the areas to be benchmarked and appropriate milestones have been identified, these should be related to the parameters that can be measured, and include the influences on those measures.

Several ideas were put forward for measuring the review process, which would allow the monitoring of performance of individual applications, as well as comparisons between different authorities (Table 12.1). External influences on these measures, such as guidelines or dialogue, also need to be identified, including factors that may not be easy to quantify but may influence an authority's performance. The latter include:

> Guidelines/ decisions/ rules
> Patient and market accessibility
> Acceptability by other jurisdictions
> Quality of submission

Attention was drawn to the importance of making sure that measures were consistent and comparable. As an example, time taken must be reported in calendar days or working days but not a mixture of the two. It is also essential to identify an authority's financial year as this may influence measures at a certain time of the year. Whether measures are recorded continuously or annually is therefore a further consideration.

It was agreed that there was a need to separate assessment time and process (i.e. non-scientific) time although it was recognised that information on process time alone is not currently available. The analogy was drawn with the lawyer's office where the client is only charged for the time spent working on their case. A better understanding of how much of the approval time is taken up by the assessment rather than bureaucracy would allow a comparison, between regions, of the duration of the scientific review.

138

Table 12.1 Parameters that can be measured or can influence review performance

| For individual compounds | Measures/influences |
|---|---|
| Total approval time | Primary scientific review time<br>Company response time<br>Total approval time: company response time |
| Time spent per activity | Actual assessment time: *time during which the compound is actually being assessed by a reviewer*<br>Process time: *time during which the compound is not being assessed by the reviewer but the compound has not been approved*<br>Company response time: *time a company takes to respond to questions raised by the authority* |
| Resources utilised | Number of staff involved in review<br>Cost of process |
| Dialogue | Prior to the review: *type and frequency*<br>During the review |
| *For individual agencies* | |
| Productivity per unit time | Number of NMEs/abridged applications reviewed<br>Number withdrawn/rejected/accepted<br>Number priority/standard review process |

**Targets**

When setting targets their definition must be clear as well as the applications to which they refer (e.g. NME, priority status). Although no specific targets were identified during the workshop, some participants contended that there is only one target, the one set by the legal framework of the country concerned. Therefore any change would have to occur at a political level. While recognising that authorities have their own national obligations and control mechanisms, transparency amongst the agencies would allow identification of performance issues and thus stimulate debate. Transparency was seen as a potential target, as well as the rate of improvement in desired outcomes within individual agencies. This latter point raises the value of targets, with both industry and regulators believing that targets can be performance drivers so long as they are realistic. The ability to set targets not only allows an agency to be congratulated when targets are met but also enables them to be challenged regarding the reasons targets are not met. More importantly, this provides an opportunity for improving the process.

### Paradigm shifts

Issues relating to re-engineering the review process were also raised for discussion during the syndicate sessions. One concept was the on-going review, where individual components of the overall data set would be forwarded, as available, by the sponsor to the agency, rather than waiting until the dossier was complete. The pros and cons of such an approach were provided by FDA representatives who have had experience of such a rolling review. The most obvious benefit is that the review process starts earlier. An examination of early data sets impacts on the ability to grant approval. The downside is that if clinical data do not meet expectations or the application does not come to fruition then this investment of time and resources has been wasted. In addition, there is no clear "clock-start" so that review times can appear very long There may, however, be a place for a hybrid system where there are clear definitions for the clock start and stop, key parameters are controlled and there is a clear indication that clinical data would support the initiation of a review.

To assure data quality, the possibility of in-process controls taking place within the company or contract research organisatior was suggested. This could reduce some of the checking and validation that has to be performed by an agency. Sponsors would require certification, similar to good manufacturing practices, but this kind of activity would be based on a mutual trust.

140

**Future consideration**

The clear message from these sessions was that there is value in having performance measures and targets for the review process. In addition, the activities involving the authority prior to and post review should also be benchmarked. However, it was not possible at this meeting to define performance measures and set targets for the authorities. This situation arose because of differences in practices and legal obligations as well as a lack of understanding of the similarities and differences between the review processes of each authority. Both industry and regulatory representatives acknowledge that since there will be simultaneous submissions in the future and, essentially, authorities will be reviewing the same data set, not only could performance be compared but also the utilisation of resources questioned. In order to have systems that can be compared in the future, a number of actions are required. These can be grouped into three areas: record regulatory activity; publish data on cycle times; and compare performances across agencies (Table 12.2).

*Record regulatory activities*

So that performance measures and targets for the review process can be set and ultimately compared across authorities, there must be commitment to the continued measurement and recording of core milestones throughout the review process for each marketing authorisation submission. However, to allow for comparisons there needs to be agreement on comparable milestones. Only three common milestones were identified as being consistent across authorities. These were the dates for: the receipt of an application, the end of the scientific assessment, and the legal authority to market a product. However, benchmarking validation was also seen as important. Recording the amount of time each dossier spends in the three main review activities of active assessment, process time and time spent waiting for companies to respond to questions raised by the regulatory authority, is critical. These records will identify potential differences between authorities, although record-

141

**Table 12.2 Suggested actions necessary for regulatory authorities' performance to be compared**

*Record regulatory activities*
   Monitor and record cycle times between agreed core milestones
   Measure assessment time, process time and company down time

*Publish data on cycle times*
   Encourage transparency by all authorities
   Provide feedback to industry and agencies

*Compare performance across agencies*
   Create a database on global review activities
   Promote discussion on milestones
   Monitor progress of simultaneously submitted dossiers through
   different regulatory authorities
   Provide direction and debate in order to further a common
   understanding

ing other possible milestones may be required for these times to be accurately assessed.

*Publish data on cycle times*

Increased transparency by the authorities in terms of publishing cycle times for each compound between core milestones, as well as the proportion of time each compound spends in the three main review activities was encouraged. This information will give a measure of how well an authority is performing. It will also provide companies with a better knowledge of when questions on their dossier may be raised and how long their compound is likely to spend in the review process. This will also ensure the public knows how long it takes to have new medicines approved. More importantly, such information will promote discussion on authorities' core activities and will allow the identification of performance issues. Supporting data will, however, also be required to address the issue of whether differences are due to processes or resources.

*Compare performance across agencies*

It was recommended that a database of global review activities should be created, with agencies being benchmarked based on comparable milestones. This database could then be utilised to compare performances across agencies in terms of time between comparable milestones and activities. Such a database would also allow simultaneously submitted dossiers to be tracked and compared through the different systems. Ultimately, a greater appreciation of how each regulatory system works would lead to a common understanding between authorities in the future.

## Conclusion

In the time available, the groups were not able to define mutually agreeable performance measures and specific targets. However, it was clear that increased transparency of the cycle times between agreed core milestones, and the creation of a database of global review activities would be the first steps in systematically measuring review activities. These could lead to the setting of realistic targets based on actual performance and ultimately the identification of strategies for improved review processes.

## What are the appropriate measures of the quality of the review?

### Introduction

Before attempting to identify ways of assessing the quality of a review, one of the syndicate groups focused on why there is such interest in quality. From industry's viewpoint the reasons include consistency, transparency and adequacy in the review process coupled with a desire for feedback. For their part, regulators have been mandated to take the right decision on behalf of the public health and it is important to continue to live up to that premiss while trying to increase efficiency. At the same time regulators should be willing to respond to legitimate critique not only with regard to procedures and efficiency but also in relation to industry's requirements. There was a general feeling that unless the issue of quality is addressed now it will become increasingly difficult to define what is a reasonable review time. For regulators, therefore, the issue of quality is one of increasing importance.

### What is quality?

The breadth of discussion within and between the syndicate groups underlined the difficulty in arriving at a straightforward answer to this question. First of all, it is difficult to differentiate between the quality of the dossier and the quality of the review. Secondly, some argued that the quality of the review, that is the assessment, should be separated from the quality of the final decision. Thirdly, as chairman of one of the syndicate groups, Dr Murray Lumpkin (CDER, FDA) expressed the view that efficiency and quality are inextricably bound to each other. They are the 'ying and yang' of both the review process and of the process used by industry to compile the application.

Suggested components of a quality review are listed in Table 12.3. These form the baseline but there is a need for reasonable adaptation and flexibility as well, otherwise the review process

**Table 12.3 Components of a quality review**

- Right format
- Scientifically sound
- Legally and scientifically consistent
- Procedurally predictable
- Within time targets

would be little more than rules and checklists with no room for judgement. An adequate review should not only embrace the listed components but should conform to the principles of critical appraisal; the reviewer can provide added value to the review through their own insight and experience.

### Building in quality

There was some discussion in one of the syndicate groups on how, on the industry side, quality can be built into the review process. There is no doubt that improving the quality of the documentation submitted to the regulators, through the use of SOPs (standard operating procedures) and quality assurance checks of both the data and the presentation, can have a marked impact on the review process.

However, the focus of interest related to quality assurance (QA) within the regulatory agencies. Most believe that agencies now have no choice – they must have QA mechanisms in place. They too need SOPs and quality control (QC) measures, with assessment guidelines or codes of good review practices (Table 12.4). One group suggested that a dedicated officer or 'quality manager' may be the only way to ensure the quality of an assessment.

Training was seen as an important way to build in quality, requiring not only a greater emphasis on the training of assessors but also of the advisory committees. In addition, most participants saw the need for feedback on the quality measures both to the assessors, including those in training, and to the sponsor. Industry

**Table 12.4  How to build quality into the review process**

---

- Quality assurance measures: QC, SOPs, Internal Audits etc.

- Training based on:   EU assessment report guideline
                       Good review practices
                       Technical guidelines

- Feedback on QA measures:   to sponsors
                             to assessors

---

representatives expressed a strong desire for feedback on the quality of the sponsor's own assessment as reflected in the expert report or summary within the dossier.

### Measuring and achieving quality

It is difficult to find tangible measures of quality, particularly quality of the scientific assessment. In one group congruence and conformity were seen as the keys – congruence between assessors, congruence between the sponsor's assessment and that of the regulator, and conformity with appropriate guidelines. Both groups acknowledged that peer review has an important part to play even if at present it is not formalised into review procedures.

Peer review occurs internally at different levels within the agency, for example, through the process of signing off. External advisory groups also provide an element of peer review and in Europe, in particular, colleagues from other regulatory agencies now provide an added dimension of importance. Under the new European procedures not only will the quality of the assessment have an impact within the national agency but it will also influence how the agency is regarded in a regulatory context by industry throughout Europe. It was suggested that each reviewer should be able to defend his/her position with regard to the assessment before a peer review committee. In other words, there is a need for validation of the standard of a review.

Once again this points to the need for a quality management system within each agency. However, such a system is resource and time intensive and therefore presents a particular challenge to

**Table 12.5  How to achieve and maintain acceptable quality**

- External audits
- Outcome analyses
- Accreditation
- Company preferences

the smaller agencies. In addition it was recognised that any QA system has a self-developing aspect which can confound attempts to assess quality.

Possible means for achieving and maintaining acceptable quality in the review process were proposed by one group (Table 12.5) although it was recognised that implementing external audits would present the problem of how to compose the expert skills for such auditors. Many potential topics for outcome analyses were suggested, including comparisons of the assessment reports, the product information literature, the use of quality measures and so forth, across agencies.

The notion of acceptable quality begs the question 'what is acceptable?'. Concern had been expressed earlier in the meeting that in Europe there may be a movement towards too high a level of quality, with 'add-on exercises' being introduced to answer potentially unnecessary scientific questions.

### Decision quality

The regulatory process involves more than just a critical appraisal of the information presented. It also involves the decision, or outcome, which is composed of the assessment plus other factors. These factors might include the public ambience, legal issues and clinical practice in the country. Thus the net result may be a high quality decision, a low quality decision or one somewhere in between these extremes (Figure 12.1).

It was stressed that determining the quality of the decision or outcome is very much dependent on experience in time. If looking back at a decision there have been no changes over a number of

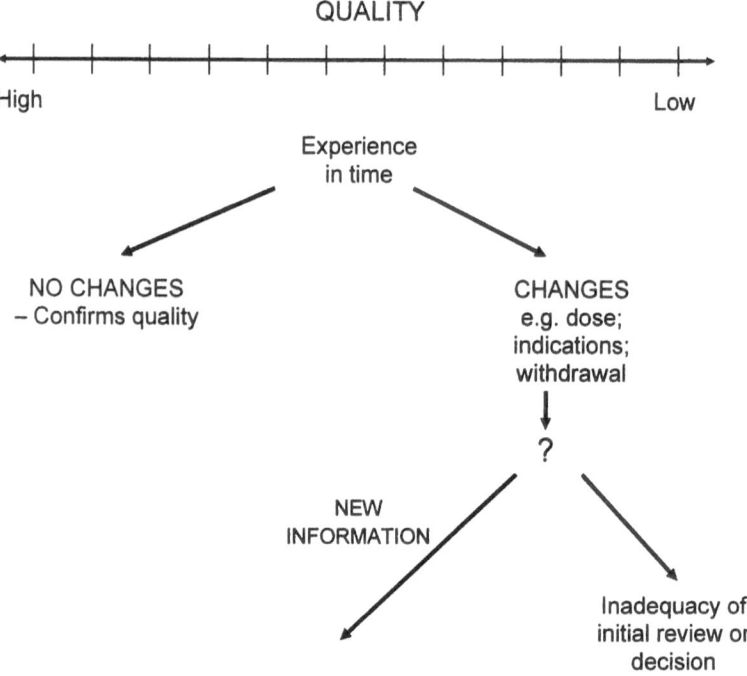

**Figure 12.1** Quality of decision/outcome

years to various aspects of the approved medicine, it appears to confirm the quality of the initial decision. If, on the other hand, there have been changes over time in the way the medicine is authorised, whether they be to the dose or indication, or indeed if the product has been withdrawn, then it appears that there may have been something amiss with the quality of the initial decision. However, the changes may have come about through new information which was not available at the time of decision making and in this case it is not possible to pass judgement on the quality of the initial decision. In other instances, however, the information may have been available from the start; this suggests the initial review or decision was inadequate.

Therefore, in any discussion on quality it is important to be aware of new information, as once new information becomes available the picture changes.

**Table 12.6  Possible measures of decision quality**

Compare between agencies:

- Results of appeals

- Differences in submitted and approved SmPC/PI

- Questions asked

- Decisions made

- Retrospective reviews – number and nature of safety changes
  number and nature of efficacy or dose changes
  withdrawals

## Measuring decision quality

There are different aspects to decision quality. It can relate to single agency decisions about either a single product or different products over time, or to multiple agency decisions about a single dossier. Among the options proposed for measuring decision quality (Table 12.6) was analysing the results of appeals against agency decisions. However, it was recognised that this approach would require a degree of transparency that may not exist at present. Retrospective reviews would probably involve only a single product, being conducted after it had been on the market for several years (at least three) or at the time the product was withdrawn.

## Comment

By the end of the syndicate sessions it was apparent that there are various tools for assessing quality, and various ones are favoured by different individuals and agencies. In general, however, they fall into two categories:

- Prospective (i.e. how to build quality into the process and how to assess that)

- Retrospective (i.e. what has been done and how it can be validated)

149

**Table 12.7 Future areas for study**

| | |
|---|---|
| 1. | Survey quality assurance measures in place in agencies, i.e. Rules/SOPs/Codes for Good Review Practice |
| 2. | Compare SmPCs/PI between agencies |
| 3. | Study results of appeals (single agency) |
| 4. | Encourage agencies to provide feedback to sponsors |
| 5. | Survey sponsors' views on the quality of assessment reports |

In the next few years, experience with using these tools will accumulate and it should then be possible to recommend which ones to use and when.

## Conclusions

A number of suggestions were made outlining areas for future study (Table 12.7). In particular, existing agencies could be surveyed to determine which quality assurance measures, such as SOPs and the methods in place for ensuring compliance, codes of good review practices or staff training, are practised at present.

As previously mentioned, studies of the differences in approved product information (PI) or summary of product characteristics (SmPC) between agencies could be undertaken. The results might reflect differences in the quality of the review, the quality of the decision or possibly reveal an issue unrelated to quality.

Agencies should be encouraged to include in their codes for good review practice the need for feedback to the sponsor, so that the sponsor is informed of the agency's view of the dossier – its presentation, ease of use and quality of the expert report or the summary. Finally, it may in time be possible to undertake surveys of sponsors' views of the quality of assessment reports from various agencies.

# Meeting participants

**Dr Eric Abadie**
Director of Registration & Clinical
   Studies
French Medicines Agency, France

**Dr Andreas Barner**
Director of Corporate Medical
   Division
Boehringer Ingelheim, Germany

**Professor Rolf Bass\*\***
Head, Human Medicines
   Evaluation Unit
European Agency for the
   Evaluation of Medicinal
   Products , UK

**Dr Joseph Bathish**
Vice President Worldwide
   Regulatory Affairs
Wyeth-Ayerst Research, USA

**Dr Eberhard Baumbauer**
Director of Research and
   Development
Verband Forschender
   Arzneimittelhersteller, Germany

**Dr André Broekmans\*\***
Executive Director
Medicines Evaluation Board,
The Netherlands

**Dr George Butler**
Head, Regulatory Group
Zeneca Pharmaceuticals, UK

**Ms Suzanne Cadden**
Director, Drug Regulatory Affairs
Glaxo Wellcome, Canada

**Mrs Frances Charlesworth**
Director, International &
   Commercial Affairs
The Association of the British
   Pharmaceutical Industry, UK

**Ms Emer Cooke**
Manager, Scientific &Regulatory
   Affairs
European Federation of
   Pharmaceutical Industries'
   Associations, Belgium

**Mrs Françoise de Cremiers**
Senior European Regulatory
   Advisor
Wyeth-Ayerst, France

**Mrs Nicole Dillier**
Drug Regulatory Affairs Associate
Novartis Pharma, Switzerland

---

†   Session Chairman
\*   Syndicate Group Chairman
\*\*  Syndicate Group Rapporteur

**Ms Emily Donnelly**
Director and Senior Vice
 President, Transnational
 Regulatory Affairs and
 Compliance
SmithKline Beecham
 Pharmaceuticals, UK

**Dr Terry Eaves**
Director, Group Development
 Operations
Glaxo Wellcome, UK

**Dr David Gannaway**
Director, Worldwide Regulatory
 Affairs
Glaxo Wellcome, UK

**Dr Alex Giaquinto**
Senior Vice President, Worldwide
 Regulatory Affairs
Schering-Plough, USA

**Dr Ken Given**
Senior Vice President, Regulatory
 Affairs
Bristol-Myers Squibb, USA

**Dr Hans-Joachim Glotz**
Head of Regulatory Affairs
Schering AG, Germany

**Dr Stef Heylen**
Vice President, International
 Registrations ·
Janssen, Belgium

**Dr Stephen Hill**
Head, International Regulatory
 Affairs
F Hoffmann-La Roche,
Switzerland

**Dr Yoshinobu Hirayama**
Manager, Clinical Trial
 Consulting Division
The Drug Organization, Japan

**Dr Carolyn Hynes**
Research Associate
Centre for Medicines Research
 International, UK

**Dr David Jefferys**
Director, Licensing Division
Medicines Control Agency, UK

**Professor Trevor Jones[†]**
Director-General
The Association of the British
 Pharmaceutical Industry, UK

**Dr Yves Juillet**
Director, Pharma Policy
Hoechst Marion Roussel, France

**Professor Gottfried Kreutz[*]**
Head, Department of
 Experimental & Clinical
 Pharmacology
Federal Institute for Drugs and
 Medical Devices, Germany

**Dr John Lechleiter**
Vice President, Development &
 Regulatory Affairs
Eli Lilly & Company, USA

**Dr Cyndy Lumley**
Associate Director
Centre for Medicines Research
 International, UK

**Dr Murray Lumpkin***
Deputy Center Director (Review
  Management)
Center for Drug Evaluation and
  Research, Food and Drug
  Administration, USA

**Dr Neil McAuslane**
Research Manager
Centre for Medicines Research
  International, UK

**Dr Michael McDonald**
Director, European Regulatory
  Team
Lilly Industries, UK

**Dr John McEwen****
Head, Clinical Evaluation Section 2
Therapeutic Goods
  Administration, Australia

**Mr Bryan Marlow**
Vice President, Regulatory Affairs
  Europe
Solvay Pharma, Germany

**Ms Vaila Marshall**
Senior Director, Regulatory
  Affairs and Clinical QA
Pfizer Central Research, UK

**Dr Hidefumi Matsui**
Senior Vice President
Yamanouchi, UK

**Dr Wim Mens**
Head, Regulatory Affairs
Organon, The Netherlands

**Mr Dann Michols***
Director General
Therapeutic Products Directorate
Health Canada, Canada

**Dr Alastair Morris**
Senior Director, International
  Regulatory Affairs
R W Johnson Pharmaceutical
  Research Institute, Switzerland

**Prof Dr Tillmann Ott**
Head, Department of
  Experimental Pharmacology &
  Toxicology
Federal Institute for Drugs and
  Medical Devices, Germany

**Ms Beth Pieterson**
Associate Director, Bureau of
  Biologics & Radiopharmaceuticals
Therapeutic Products Directorate
Health Canada, Canada

**Miss Paolo Ricci**
Senior Executive & Vice
  President, R&D and Regulatory
  Affairs
Ares Services, Switzerland

**Mrs Sandra Roberts**
Head of Regulatory Affairs
Novo Nordisk, UK

**Dr Malcolm Rogan**
Technical Director
Allergan, UK

**Dr Greg Rossi**
European Regulatory Affairs
  Specialist
Amgen, UK

**Dr Scott Russell**
Senior Research Associate
Centre for Medicines Research
  International, UK

**Mr Fernand Sauer[†]**
Executive Director
European Agency for the
  Evaluation of Medicinal
  Products , UK

**Dr Byron Scott**
Regulatory Affairs Department
Parke-Davies Pharmaceutical
  Research Institute, USA

**Professor Vittorio Silano\***
Head of Department, Medicines
Evaluation and Pharmacovigilance
Ministero della Sanità, Italy

**Dr Eve Slater**
Senior Vice President, Clinical and
  Regulatory Development
Merck Research Laboratories, USA

**Dr Christian Spilles**
Head of Regulatory Affairs
  International
Bayer, Germany

**Dr Richard Spivey**
Vice President, Worldwide
  Regulatory Affairs
Searle, USA

**Mrs Birgit Stattin**
Senior Vice President, Worldwide
  Product Development
Pharmacia & Upjohn, UK

**Professor Kjell Strandberg\*\***
Director General
Medical Products Agency, Sweden

**Dr Max Talbott**
Head, International Regulatory
  Affairs
Rhône-Poulenc Rorer, USA

**Ms Kate Thomas**
Research Associate
Centre for Medicines Research
  International, UK

**Professor Stuart Walker**
Director
Centre for Medicines Research
  International, UK

**Prof Dr Thomas Weihrauch**
Director, Medical Affairs
  International
Bayer, Germany

**Dr Roger Williams**
Associate Director for Science &
  Medical Affairs
Center for Drug Evaluation and
  Research, Food and Drug
  Administration, USA

**Dr Manuel Zahn**
Head of Regulatory Support
Knoll, Germany

**Dr Kathryn Zoon[†]**
Director
Center for Biologics Evaluation
  and Research, Food and Drug
  Administration, USA

154

# Glossary

| | |
|---|---|
| ABPI | The Association of the British Pharmaceutical Industry |
| ADEC | Australian Drug Evaluation Committee |
| ADR | Adverse drug reaction |
| AR | Assessment Report |
| ATS | Application track system |
| | |
| BfArM | Bundesinstitut fur Arzneimittel und Medizinprodukte (Federal Institute for Drugs and Medical Devices) |
| | |
| CAMM | Commission d'Authorisation de Mise sur le Marché (France) |
| CANDA | Computer-assisted new drug application |
| CBER | Center for Biologics Evaluation and Research (FDA, USA) |
| CDER | Center for Drug Evaluation and Research (FDA, USA) |
| CPAC | Central Pharmaceutical Affairs Council (MHW, Japan) |
| CPMP | Committee for Proprietary Medicinal Products (EU) |
| CSM | Committee on Safety of Medicines (UK) |
| CVMP | Committee for Veterinary Medicinal Products (EU) |
| | |
| DART | Drug Applications for Registration Tracking (Australia) |
| DG | Directorate General (EU) |
| DSMB | Data and Safety Monitoring Boards (FDA, USA) |
| | |
| EC | European Community |
| EFPIA | European Federation of Pharmaceutical Industries' Associati( |
| EFTA | European Free Trade Association |
| ELA | Establishment Licence Application |
| EMEA | European Agency for the Evaluation of Medicinal Products |
| EPAR | European Public Assessment Report |
| ETOMEP | European Technical Office for Medicinal Products |
| EU | European Union |
| | |
| FDA | Food and Drug Administration (USA) |
| FMA | Agence du Médicament (France) |

GCP          Good clinical practice
GLP          Good laboratory practice
GMP          Good manufacturing practice
GPMSP        Good post-marketing surveillance practice
GRP          Good review practice

ICH          International Conference on Harmonization
IMH          Ministry of Health (Italy)
IND          Investigational new drug
IS           Information systems
IT           Information technology

JRC          Joint Research Centre (Europe)

MA           Marketing Authorisation
MAA          Marketing Authorisation Application
MCA          Medicines Control Agency (UK)
MEB          Medicines Evaluation Board (The Netherlands)
MHW          Ministry of Health & Welfare (Japan)
MPA          Medical Products Agency (Sweden)
MR           Mutual Recognition (EU)
MRC          Managed Review Committee (CBER, USA)
MRL          Maximum residue limits
MRP          Managed review process (CBER, USA)
MS           Member State (EU)

NAS          New active substance
NDA          New Drug Application
NIH          National Institute of Health (USA)
NME          New molecular entity

OECD         Organization for Economic Cooperation and Development

PAB          Pharmaceutical Affairs Bureau (MHW, Japan)
PAL          Pharmaceutical Affairs Law (Japan)
PDUFA        Prescription Drug User Fee Act (USA)
PER          Pharmaceutical Evaluation Report (EU)
PI           Product information
PMS          Post-marketing surveillance

QA           Quality assurance
QC           Quality control

| | |
|---|---|
| RAA | Registration Approval Application |
| REGO | Re-inventing Government (USA) |
| RMS | Reference Member State (EU) |
| | |
| S&E | Safety and efficacy |
| SmPC | Summary of product characteristics |
| SOP | Standard operating procedure |
| | |
| TGA | Therapeutic Goods Administration (Australia) |
| TGAL | Therapeutic Goods Administration Laboratories (Australia) |
| TPD | Therapeutic Products Directorate (Canada) |
| | |
| UNESCO | United Nations Educational, Scientific, and Cultural Organization |
| UPL | User package leaflet |
| | |
| WHO | World Health Organization |

# Index